PENGUIN STUDENTS' GRAMMAR OF ENGLISH EXERCISES

Susan Firman & René Bosewitz

Penguin Books

PENGUIN BOOKS

Published by the Penguin Group
27 Wrights Lane, London W8 5TZ, England
Viking Penguin Inc., 40 West 23rd Street, New York, New York 10010, USA
Penguin Books Australia Ltd, Ringwood, Victoria, Australia
Penguin Books Canada Ltd, 2801 John Street, Markham, Ontario, Canada L3R 1B4
Penguin Books (NZ) Ltd, 182–190 Wairau Road, Auckland 10, New Zealand

Penguin Books Ltd, Registered Offices: Harmondsworth, Middlesex, England

First published 1988

Set in Linotron 202 10/15 pt Plantin Medium

Reproduced, printed and bound in Great Britain by
Hazell Watson & Viney Limited
Member of BPCC plc
Aylesbury, Bucks, England

Designed by Jacky Wedgwood
Illustrated by Sean MacGarry

CONTENTS

1 NOUNS

BIRD'S EYE BOX: Nouns

People who live in glass **houses** shouldn't throw **stones**.	→	singular and regular/irregular plurals (Exercise 1)
Have you seen my **sunglasses** anywhere?	→	compound nouns (Exercise 2)
He's making good **progress**.	→	nouns generally used in the singular
Have you washed my **jeans**?	→	nouns generally used in the plural (Exercise 3)
I'll see you at **Mary's** party. I think he's at a **directors'** meeting.	→	possession: singular and plural (Exercise 4)

EXERCISE 1

Complete the following table with the correct noun (singular or plural). The first one has been done for you.

	SINGULAR	PLURAL		SINGULAR	PLURAL
1	glass	**glasses**	9		knives
2	secretary		10	key	
3		people	11	child	
4		shoes	12		boxes
5	fish		13	tomato	
6		ladies	14	photograph	
7	tooth		15		bushes
8	policeman		16		feet

EXERCISE 2

Combine a word from box A with a word from box B to form a compound noun. Then use the nouns to complete the sentences below, making the noun plural where necessary. The first one has been done for you.

A	B
ash ear arm hand head house news note rain tooth	bag book brush coat chair line paper ring tray work

1 Hadn't you better take your **raincoat**? It's awfully cloudy.

2 Have you seen today's ______________? The Prime Minister's resigned!

3 I get the shopping on Thursdays and do all the ______________ on Fridays, so the weekend's free for the family.

4 Could you pass me that ______________? I want to have a cigarette.

5 What a pretty pair of ______________! Are those diamonds?

6 Have you finished with the ______________? I want to see what's on television tonight.

7 Now, you've got your razor and your shaving-cream, haven't you? What about your ______________?

8 Why don't you sit in the ______________? You'll be more comfortable.

9 If you pass me my ______________, I'll give you the money now.

10 It's a good idea to write down new vocabulary in a ______________. Then you can refer to it later.

EXERCISE 3

Complete the following by putting a circle round the correct word in the brackets.

Example: I must get my (hair / hairs) cut.

1 Could you give me some (information/informations) about trains to Edinburgh?

2 Where have I put my (glass/glasses)? I can't read a thing!

3 Put it on the (scale/scales) so I can see how much it weighs.

4 I can't come out tonight. I've got a lot of (homework/homeworks) to do.

5 You'll find your clean (pyjama/pyjamas) in the cupboard.

6 They've got some lovely (furniture/furnitures), but just look at the price!

7 If you spoke to your solicitor about it, I'm sure he'd give you some (advice/advices).

8 Could you pass me the (scissor/scissors)? I can't cut this with a knife.

EXERCISE 4

Choose the correct word (a, b or c) to complete the sentence and write the appropriate letter in the box. The first one has been done for you.

1 You can't sit there. That's ______________ place.
(a) Alison (b) Alison's (c) Alisons' [b]

2 Could you take these books to the ______________ Room, please?
(a) Teacher (b) Teacher's (c) Teachers' [ ]

3 We're going to a ______________ party this afternoon.
(a) children (b) children's (c) childrens' [ ]

4 Have you seen the ______________ keys anywhere?
(a) car (b) car's (c) cars' [ ]

5 That's Mrs Davies, the ______________ wife.
(a) doctor (b) doctor's (c) doctors' [ ]

6 I'm borrowing my ______________ car while they're away.
(a) parent (b) parent's (c) parents' [ ]

7 I must buy some new ______________ curtains.
(a) bedroom (b) bedroom's (c) bedrooms' [ ]

8 That's ______________ bag, isn't it?
(a) Terry (b) Terry's (c) Terrys' [ ]

2 ARTICLES

BIRD'S EYE BOX: Articles

		THE DEFINITE ARTICLE
The girl who lives next door	⟶	a specified noun (Exercises 1, 2 and 7)
The earth travels round **the** sun.	⟶	a unique object (Exercises 1, 2 and 7)
The French, **the** rich	⟶	an adjective used as a noun (Exercises 1 and 7)
The best book I've ever read	⟶	superlatives (Exercises 1 and 7)
		ZERO ARTICLE
Women live longer than men.	⟶	plural nouns in general statements (Exercises 1, 2 and 7)
Tom, Sweden, Friday, Easter, summer	⟶	names, countries, days, festivals, seasons (Exercises 1 and 7)
Time passes quickly.	⟶	abstract nouns (Exercises 1 and 2)
		THE INDEFINITE ARTICLE
a man, **an** idea	⟶	singular nouns, not specified (Exercises 3 and 7)
Twice **a** day	⟶	expressions of frequency (Exercise 4)
£1.50 **a** metre	⟶	measurements (Exercises 5 and 7)
What **an** awful shock!	⟶	exclamations (Exercise 6)

EXERCISE 1

Complete the following dialogues by putting **the** *into the spaces only where necessary.*

1 'Excuse me. Can you tell me where (a) ______ nearest garage is?'
'It's on (b) ______ main road, just after (c) ______ supermarket.'

2 'Who's that girl over there talking to (a) _______ man with red hair?'
'Oh, that's Sandra. She's one of (b) _______ girls I work with. She only started (c) _______ week before last.'

3 'Did you have a good holiday?'
'Yes, it was one of (a) _______ best we've ever had. (b) _______ hotel was comfortable, (c) _______ food was excellent and even (d) _______ beaches were clean. We're going back (e) _______ next summer.'

4 'Do you think (a) _______ men are better drivers than (b) _______ women?'
'Not necessarily. Some of (c) _______ worst drivers I know are (d) _______ men.'

5 'What's on at (a) _______ cinema? Anything interesting?'
'No. There's only a musical or a Western. We've seen (b) _______ Western before, and I don't like (c) _______ musicals very much.'

6 'Who put (a) _______ first man into (b) _______ space? (c) _______ America or (d) _______ Russia?'
'(e) _______ Russia. But (f) _______ Americans were first on (g) _______ moon.'

7 'Are you voting for (a) _______ Government in (b) _______ next election?'
'Certainly not. This Government has only made (c) _______ rich richer and (d) _______ poor poorer. And they've done nothing to help (e) _______ unemployed find (f) _______ jobs!'

8 'I don't agree that (a) _______ honesty is always (b) _______ best policy. Do you?'
'Definitely not. (c) _______ diplomacy is sometimes more important.'

EXERCISE 2

Complete the following speech by putting **the** *into the spaces only where necessary (not in every sentence).*

'We in (1) _______ West are very lucky. How often do we experience (2) _______ real poverty, (3) _______ oppression or (4) _______ natural disasters? (5) _______ life for us is fairly easy compared with (6) _______ life led by millions all over (7) _______ world. I have travelled far and wide and (8) _______ poverty I have seen in some countries is unimaginable. Every day (9) _______ people die from (10) _______ starvation and (11) _______ diseases caused by (12) ______ starvation. (13) ______ people in these countries need (14) ______ food and (15) ______ medicine urgently, and they are asking us for (16) ______ help. But we need (17) ______ money: your money. We cannot buy (18) ______ food they need, nor provide (19) ______ medicine they require without (20) ______ money you give today. So, please, give generously. Thank you.'

EXERCISE 3

*Put **a** or **an** before each of the following.*

1 ______ hotel

2 ______ hour

3 ______ unusual situation

4 ______ university education

5 ______ unidentified flying object

6 ______ horrible dream

7 ______ honest man

8 ______ union official

EXERCISE 4

A housewife talks about her family. Read what she says and then complete the exercise below. (You must work out how often each thing happens.) The first one has been done for you.

I take the dog for a walk every morning and evening and I go to keep-fit classes on Mondays, Wednesdays and Thursdays. So, as you can see, I get plenty of exercise! I've got two children. Tom, the elder, works abroad, but he comes home every three months or so. We always get at least a couple of letters from him every month. Sally, my daughter, has just got a boyfriend. He always phones her at eight o'clock in the evening and they talk for hours! We nearly always go away on holiday when school finishes, at Christmas, Easter and in the summer. Sometimes it's only for a few days and sometimes longer. I think we're basically a very close family.

1 She takes the dog for a walk **twice a day**.

2 She goes to keep-fit classes ____________________.

3 Tom comes home ____________________.

4 They get a letter from Tom at least ____________________.

5 Sally's boyfriend always phones her ____________________.

6 They go away on holiday ____________________.

EXERCISE 5

Using the information in the shopping list, complete the sentences below. The first one has been done for you. (Note: £1 = 100p)

5 kilos of potatoes	60p
2 loaves of bread	70p
½ dozen eggs	79p
3 pints of milk	69p
2 litres of orange juice	98p
4 cans of beer	£1.20
500 grams of butter	£1.11
1.5 litres of wine	£4.50

1 The potatoes were **12p a kilo**.

2 The bread was ______ a loaf.

3 The eggs were ______ a dozen.

4 The milk was ____________.

5 The orange juice was ____________.

6 The beer was ____________.

7 The butter was ____________.

8 The wine was ____________.

EXERCISE 6

Complete the exclamations with **a** *or* **an** *only where necessary (not in every sentence).*

Examples: What an awful shock! What beautiful flowers!

1 What ______ lovely day!

2 What ______ nice people!

3 What ______ awful experience!

4 What ______ terrible noise!

5 What ______ dreadful weather!

6 What ______ well-behaved children!

7 What ______ good idea!

8 What ______ interesting story!

9 What ______ sad news!

10 What ______ idiotic thing to do!

EXERCISE 7

Complete the news items with **the, a** *or* **an** *only where necessary.*

Good evening. Here is (1) ______ nine o'clock news.

(2) ______ Prime Minister arrived in Washington this morning for (3) ______ talks with (4) ______ American President. (5) ______ talks are expected to start in (6) ______ morning.

(7) ______ Government has promised to give (8) ______ quarter of (9) ______ million pounds to help (10) ______ homeless in London. (11) ______ recent survey has shown that (12) ______ number of people without (13) ______ homes has doubled in (14) ______ last two years.

(15) _______ man was arrested in London this evening after (16) _______ 100 mile (17) _______ hour car chase along (18) _______ M4 motorway. (19) _______ man has, so far, not been named.

(20) _______ lorry containing (21) _______ dangerous chemicals was stolen from outside (22) _______ factory in Epping over (23) _______ weekend. (24) _______ spokesman for (25) _______ factory said (26) _______ chemicals were highly poisonous.

From midnight tonight (27) _______ petrol will cost (28) _______ extra 1p (29) _______ litre. (30) _______ rise is caused by (31) _______ present high price of (32) _______ oil in (33) _______ Middle East.

(34) _______ eighty-year-old man has become (35) _______ oldest person to cross (36) _______ Atlantic alone. Sam Taylor, from New York, arrived in Plymouth last night.

3 PRONOUNS

BIRD'S EYE BOX: Pronouns

I'll see **you** later.	⟶	personal pronouns (object) (Exercises 1 and 9)
Hey! That's **mine**!	⟶	possessive pronouns (Exercise 1)
I can't find **my** car keys.	⟶	possessive adjectives (Exercises 1 and 9)
She's staying with some friends **of hers**.	⟶	double possessive (Exercise 1)
These flowers are for you. **That's** mine!	⟶	demonstrative adjectives/ pronouns (Exercises 2 and 9)
He hurt **himself** quite badly.	⟶	reflexive pronouns (Exercises 3, 4 and 9)
They disliked **each other/one another** on sight.	⟶	reciprocal pronouns (Exercises 4 and 9)
Isn't he the man **whose** photo was in the paper?	⟶	relative pronouns (Exercises 5, 6, 7 and 9)
There's **no one** there.	⟶	indefinite pronouns (Exercises 8 and 9)
Didn't she say **anything else**?	⟶	indefinite pronouns + **else** (Exercises 8 and 9)

EXERCISE 1

David Garrick, Roger Warner and Bill Matthews have just interviewed several applicants for a job. Complete the following discussion by putting a circle round the correct pronoun or adjective in the brackets.

Example: The final decision is (me / my / (mine))

DAVID: Well, gentlemen, that's the last applicant, and now it's up to (1) (us/our/ours) to make a decision. It seems to (2) (me/my/mine) that there are only two possibilities: Jane Barratt and Michael Smith.

However, as (3) (them/their/theirs) qualifications are equally good and they've both got a lot of experience, it's difficult to choose between (4) (them/their/theirs). So, I'd like to hear (5) (you/your/yours) opinions first. Roger?

ROGER: Oh, I'd definitely give the job to (6) (she/her/hers). I liked (7) (she/her/hers) enthusiasm and felt (8) (she/her/hers) ideas were more up to date than (9) (he/his/him). To be honest, I was rather disappointed in (10) (he/his/him). I found (11) (he/his/him) rather dull. Well, that's (12) (me/my/mine) opinion. What's (13) (you/your/yours), Bill?

BILL: I don't really agree with (14) (you/your/yours), Roger. I got the impression she was rather neurotic. She reminded me of a friend of (15) (us/our/ours) who is very unreliable. I'd give (16) (he/his/him) the job and not (17) (she/her/hers). Don't forget, (18) (he/his/him) references are much better than (19) (she/her/hers).

ROGER: References! Who takes any notice of references! If I remember correctly, (20) (me/my/mine) weren't very good either, and I doubt if (21) (you/your/yours) were much better, Bill!

BILL: Speak for yourself, Roger! Anyway, it's no business of (22) (you/your/yours)!

DAVID: Gentlemen, if we could get back to discussing the candidates. Now, personally, I agree with . . .

EXERCISE 2

Complete the following with **this, that, these** *or* **those**. *The first one has been done for you.*

1 These are very pretty, aren't they? I particularly like <u>**this**</u> one. Don't you?

2 Who's that man talking to ______ people over there?

3 I like this bag, but it's rather expensive. How much is ______ one in the window?

4 This is my husband, Robert, and ______ are my children, Tom and Helen.

5 That knife's not very sharp. Here, use ______ one.

6 The postman's just been. This one's for me and all ______ are for you. Here you are.

7 These clothes over here are in the sale, madam, but ______ on the other side aren't.

8 Those children next door are dreadful, aren't they? And ______ boy Nigel is the worst!

EXERCISE 3

*Read the following pieces of conversation overheard at a party. Fill in the spaces with the correct reflexive pronoun (**myself, yourself,** etc.) only where necessary (not every time). The first one has been done for you.*

1 'Oh, it's nothing much really. I cut **myself** when I was opening a tin.'

2 'My eldest son's gone hitch-hiking in France. I suppose he can take care of ____________, but I'm not very happy about it.'

3 'We had a few days' holiday in Morocco last month. We both thoroughly enjoyed ____________ it.'

4 'Of course, we miss the boys now they've left home, but I must admit we do appreciate having more time to ____________.'

5 'Thanks for coming to the party, Tony. I hope you're enjoying ____________.'

6 'Well, I must say I thought she behaved ____________ terribly badly under the circumstances.'

7 'Come on, everybody. There's plenty to eat and drink, so please help ____________.'

8 'We've left the children with Jim's mother. I only hope they're behaving ____________!'

EXERCISE 4

*Complete the following two letters with the correct reflexive pronoun (**myself, yourself,** etc.) or **each other/one another**.*

Examples: They haven't spoken to **each other/one another** since they quarrelled.
They should be ashamed of **themselves**.

Dear Rosemary,

You'll never guess who I heard from last week. Julie Saunders! We haven't seen (1) ________________ for at least two years! Anyway, she's invited us to spend the weekend at her house in Sussex. I only hope Bill and Andrew get on with (2) ________________ and that the children behave (3) ________________!

I'll tell you all about it in my next letter. Meanwhile, take care of (4) ________________.

With love,
Debbie

Dear Rosemary,

The weekend with Julie Saunders was quite successful. At least, Bill and I enjoyed (5) ________________; Bill and Andrew liked (6) ________________ immediately and spent most of the weekend discussing sport. Unfortunately, our children and Julie's two took an instant dislike to (7) ________________! However, the weather was fine, so they were able to amuse (8) ________________ in the garden, although they wouldn't play with (9) ________________.

Of course, Julie and I had a lot to say to (10) ________________, and the time just flew by. But we hope to meet (11) ________________ in London one day. Why don't you come too? Anyway, in the meantime, look after (12) ________________.

With love,
Debbie

EXERCISE 5

Complete the following newspaper article by choosing the correct pronoun from the box below. Use each pronoun twice only.

who whom whose which

Actress Buried in Hollywood

The actress Lilian Bell, (1) ________ died last week, was buried today in Hollywood. Miss Bell, (2) ________ career in films lasted more than forty years, was one of the great stars of the 1940s. Her most successful role was Catherine the Great in *The Russian Empress*, (3) ________ was directed by her first husband, Daniel Steinberg, from (4) ________ she was divorced in 1952. She later married the actor Peter Becker, with (5) ________ she made several films before his death in 1969. Hilary Marshall, (6) ________ biography of Miss Bell was published last year, said, 'She was a talented actress (7) ________ knew exactly what the public wanted. Her death is the end of an era (8) ________ produced some of the finest actors in the history of the cinema.'

EXERCISE 6

You are showing holiday photos to a friend. Join the two sentences to make one sentence by using **who, which** *or* **whose** *only where necessary. Sometimes other changes in the sentence will be required.*

Examples: That's the courier. She looked after us.
That's the courier who looked after us.

That's the beach. We went to it every day.
That's the beach we went to every day.

1 That's the Smith family. They had the room next to ours.

2 That's Señor Bueno. His daughter worked in the hotel.

3 That's the Tropicana Disco. We went to it a couple of times.

4 That's the local bookshop. It sold English newspapers.

5 That's the Pablo family. We met them on the beach.

6 That's Señora Pablo. Her brother works in London.

7 That's Roberto, the waiter. He showed us how to dance flamenco.

8 That's the hotel cat. It used to follow us to the beach.

EXERCISE 7

Read the following news items and then join each of the pairs of sentences to make one sentence by using **who, which, whose** *or* **whom**. *Sometimes there may be more than one acceptable answer.*

Example: Two youths have been fined £500 for starting a fire. They both have criminal records.
Two youths, who both have criminal records, have been fined £500 for starting a fire.

1 Heavy snow has blocked most roads in the north of Scotland. It fell unexpectedly during the night.

2 Cardinal Onzo of Brazil left from Heathrow this morning. The Archbishop of Canterbury had talks with him earlier this week.

3 Amateur radio enthusiast Paul Little saved the lives of nine Spanish seamen last night. He heard the SOS signal on his transmitter.

4 Simon Walsh, twenty-two, appeared at Manchester Crown Court today, charged with driving without a licence. His father is the Conservative M.P. for Lower Trauton.

5 A priceless seventeenth-century painting has been discovered in a house in Berkshire. It was stolen over twenty-five years ago.

6 Mr and Mrs Andrew Baker have received more than £200,000 compensation from their local council. Their house was demolished by mistake.

7 The famous 1920s beauty Nancy Loughborough has died in her sleep at eighty-two. The well-known song 'Beautiful' was written for her.

8 And finally, Mrs Brenda Tyler has been nominated Slimmer of the Year. She lost more than thirty-five kilos in six months.

EXERCISE 8

*Complete the following sentences with the correct pronoun (***someone/body, something***, etc.), using* **else** *where necessary.*

Example: I couldn't get any small tomatoes, but I got **everything else** on the list you gave me.

1 Do you think you could ask ____________________ to help you? I'm rather busy at the moment.

2 Has ____________________ seen my bag? I'm sure I left it on the table.

3 There's not much on television tonight. The film at nine o'clock might be OK, but there's ________________ worth watching.

4 Derek's late again! Honestly, if ________________ can get here on time, why can't he?

5 Do you want ________________ to eat or drink, or shall I ask for the bill?

6 I've done ________________ you asked me to do, Mr Elgood, so is it all right if I go home now?

7 Look, it's rather confidential. So, although I've told you, I don't want ________________ to know. OK?

8 Come outside a minute, Jane. There's ________________ I want to tell you.

9 Alice was there and so was Philip, but ________________ came! So, as you can imagine, it was a pretty awful party!

10 Well, the police asked a lot of questions, but I couldn't help them, as I knew ________________ about the people upstairs.

11 I've been to the bank, collected the dry-cleaning and paid the electricity bill. But I'm sure there was ________________ I had to do.

12 ________________ phoned you earlier, but he didn't leave his name.

EXERCISE 9

Complete the following speech by putting a circle round the correct pronoun or adjective in the brackets.

Ladies and gentlemen, could I have (1) (you/your/yours) attention for a moment? As you know, (2) (this/that/these/those) is a very sad occasion for all of (3) (us/our/ours), because we have to say goodbye to Duncan Saunders, (4) (who/whom/whose) retires today after twenty-five years with the company.

Duncan has been here longer than (5) (someone else/anyone/anyone else), and we will miss (6) (he/his/him) very much. He has always been an enthusiastic worker, (7) (who/whom/whose) sense of humour cheered (8) (someone/anyone/everyone) up, especially on Monday mornings! He is a man I admire and respect enormously, even though, as he well knows, we haven't always seen eye-to-eye with (9) (ourselves/each other/us). And I'm sure he remembers (10) (this/that/these/those) arguments as well as I do!

Duncan, if you look at the contribution you have made to the company, you can be proud of (11) (you/yours/yourself). And to show (12) (us/our/ours) appreciation, we would like to give you (13) (anything/something/nothing else) to remember (14) (us/our/ours) by. And I am sure I'm not just speaking for (15) (me/each other/myself) but for (16) (anyone else/someone else/everyone else) too when I wish you and your wife a very happy retirement.

4 QUESTION WORDS

BIRD'S EYE BOX: Question words

What? Who? Where? When? Why? Which? Whose? How many/much/often/far/long? **What** did you do? **Where** did you go?	→ question words (Exercises 1, 2 and 5)
What else did you do?	→ question words + **else** (Exercise 3)
What time did you get home?	→ interrogative adjectives (Exercises 4 and 5)
What a good idea! **How** interesting!	→ exclamations (Exercise 6)

EXERCISE 1

Look at the answer in order to find the correct word or words to complete the question.

Example: '**Who** was that at the door?' 'Only the milkman.'

1 '________ did you get back?' 'Saturday night.'

2 '________ do you want to know?' 'I'm just interested, that's all.'

3 '________ do you prefer?' 'I don't really like either of them.'

4 '________ did you get home?' 'Peter gave me a lift.'

5 '________ are these?' 'They're Graham's, I think.'

6 '________ is it exactly?' 'On the outskirts of Birmingham.'

7 '________ do you see him?' 'Only once or twice a year.'

8 '________ was that?' 'I didn't hear anything.'

9 '________ is it?' 'It's me.'

10 '________ did you have to walk?' 'Only a couple of kilometres.'

EXERCISE 2

You are reading the following magazine article. Unfortunately, the page has been torn. Write down the questions you need to ask to find the missing information. The first one has been done for you.

> Another mystery is that of Lord Cluan, who disappeared in (1)
> The Cluan family, together with the children's nurse, lived in (2)
> Cluan was in serious financial trouble because of (3)
> which is probably the reason for the tragic events of that night.
> Cluan had gone out, but returned unexpectedly at about (4)
> The nurse, who was upstairs at the time, heard (5)
> and went downstairs to investigate. Cluan killed her by (6)
> It is now thought that he probably intended to murder (7)
> and not the nurse, but made a mistake because (8)
> After the murder, Cluan left and drove to (9)
> Police found his car the next morning. Inside the car they found (10)
> Cluan has never been seen since.

1 **When did Lord Cluan disappear?**

2 ______________________?

3 ______________________?

4 ______________________?

5 ______________________?

6 ______________________?

7 ______________________?

8 ______________________?

9 ______________________?

10 ______________________?

EXERCISE 3

Complete the following with the correct question word + **else***.*

Example: I'm sure he's not telling us the whole truth. **Why else** would he look so guilty?

1 I said it was confidential. But Paula knows and Brian knows. ______________ have you told?

2 Right. I've cleaned the bathroom, made the beds and tidied upstairs. ______________ would you like me to do?

3 If it's not in your bag and it's not in your pockets, ______________ could it be?

4 I'll just have to ask my father to lend me some money. ______________ can I manage till the end of the month?

5 I think they must be in serious financial trouble. ______________ would they consider selling the company?

6 I know you're free on Monday and Tuesday, but I'm a bit busy then. ______________ could you come?

EXERCISE 4

Read the following job advertisement and write down the questions you would ask an applicant. The first one has been done for you.

EXPERIENCED (1) LANGUAGE TEACHER REQUIRED FOR SCHOOL IN OXFORD

University (2) education and good qualifications (3) essential. Must speak at least two languages (4). Preference will be given to applicants who have worked in countries (5) outside the United Kingdom. An interest in sports (6) is desirable but not essential.

1 **What experience** have you had?

2 ______________ did you go to?

3 ______________?

4 ______________?

5 ______________?

6 ______________?

EXERCISE 5

Jenny is going to stay with Anne in Edinburgh. Read the following telephone conversation and write down the questions Jenny asks. The first one has been done for you. There may be more than one acceptable answer.

JENNY: (1) **Which station do the Edinburgh trains leave from?**

ANNE: King's Cross.

JENNY: (2) ______________?

ANNE: I think there's only one train an hour.

JENNY: (3) ______________?

ANNE: Every hour, on the hour. Nine o'clock, ten o'clock and so on.

JENNY: (4) ______________?

ANNE: Well, I think the Flying Scotsman's the best train. It goes at ten o'clock.

JENNY: (5) ______________?

ANNE: It takes about four and a half hours.

JENNY: (6) ____?

ANNE: I'm not sure exactly. I think a return's at least £60, but it's probably more.

JENNY: (7) ____?

ANNE: Meet me outside the station. I'll come and pick you up. I'm borrowing Peter's car for the day.

JENNY: (8) ____?

ANNE: Peter's.

JENNY: (9) ____?

ANNE: Peter? Oh, sorry. He's a friend of mine. You'll meet him while you're here.

JENNY: (10) ____?

ANNE: Oh, he's got a blue Maxi.

JENNY: (11) ____?

ANNE: Don't bring anything special. Just a pair of jeans and some walking shoes.

JENNY: (12) ____?

ANNE: Well, it depends on the weather, but I thought we might go to Loch Ness.

EXERCISE 6

Complete the following exclamations with **what** *or* **how** *and, where necessary, add* **a** *or* **an**.

Example: <u>**What a**</u> nuisance! <u>**How**</u> annoying!

1 ______________ embarrassing!

2 ______________ pity!

3 ______________ bad luck!

4 ______________ extraordinary!

5 ______________ surprise!

6 ______________ awful!

7 ______________ exciting!

8 ______________ lovely weather!

9 ______________ rude!

10 ______________ silly thing to say!

5 ADJECTIVES

BIRD'S EYE BOX: Adjectives

We need to protect **the young.**	→	adjectives used as nouns (Exercise 1)
The weather isn't very **nice.** It isn't a very **nice** day.	→	position of adjectives (Exercise 2)
She's **older** and **more experienced** than the others.	→	comparison of adjectives (Exercises 3, 4 and 6)
The latest model is also **the most expensive.**	→	superlative of adjectives (Exercises 3, 5 and 6)

EXERCISE 1

Complete the following extract from a history book by choosing from the box below. Do not use any word more than once. The first one has been done for you. Note that two words are needed in each space.

blind	good	homeless	old	poor	rich	sick	strong	unemployed
weak	wealthy	young						

Society, in those days, was divided into (1) **the rich** and (2) ______________. Life for (3) ______________ was easy. They could send their children to school and they could afford the best doctors. However, life for the vast majority was very different. There was little education for (4) ______________, no free hospital treatment for (5) ______________ and no state pensions for (6) ______________. (7) ______________, who could not find jobs, were frequently regarded as lazy, and (8) ______________, who had nowhere else to go, simply slept in the streets. It is not surprising, then, that only (9) ______________ survived. (10) ______________ rarely lived more than a few years.

EXERCISE 2

Change the order of the words to make a correct sentence.

Example: very/a/he's/man/difficult

He's a very difficult man.

1 was/meal/delicious/that/really
2 difficult/the/look/exam/terribly/doesn't
3 a/embarrassing/very/it's/situation
4 seem/children/excited/the/very/didn't
5 programme/extremely/it's/interesting/an

EXERCISE 3

Complete the table with the correct forms.

	ADJECTIVE	COMPARATIVE	SUPERLATIVE
	young	younger	(the) youngest
1		more interesting	
2	far		
3		worse	
4	easy		
5			(the) most valuable
6	thin		
7			(the) eldest/oldest
8	aggressive		
9		wider	
10	good		

EXERCISE 4

Read the following reports on two hotels. Then compare them in the space below. There may be more than one acceptable answer.

The Supercontinental	*The Glencairn Hotel*
1 **Position**: 5 minutes from city centre	1 **Position:** 15 minutes from city centre
2 **Accommodation**: 80 rooms	2 **Accommodation**: 55 rooms
3 **Price**: £60–£85 per night	3 **Price**: £40–£55 per night
4 **Facilities**: restaurant, nightclub, pool, sauna	4 **Facilities**: restaurant, bar, tennis court
5 **Food**: wide choice on menu	5 **Food**: small choice but excellent
6 **Service**: efficient but impersonal	6 **Service**: a little slow but friendly
7 **Comments**: rather noisy	7 **Comments**: quiet and comfortable

The Supercontinental	*The Glencairn Hotel*
1 **It's nearer the city centre.**	1 ______.
2 ______.	2 ______.
3 ______.	3 ______.
4 ______.	4 ______.
5 ______.	5 ______.
6 ______.	6 ______.
7 ______.	7 ______.

EXERCISE 5

Read the following notes from the diary of a mountaineer. Then complete the exercise below. The first one has been done for you.

Day 1 Didn't climb far. Fairly easy day.	*Day 4* Wind icy! Extremely cold!
Day 2 Climbed for eight hours. Very long day.	*Day 5* Weather appalling! A very bad day.
Day 3 Altitude made air thin. Very exhausting.	*Day 6* Impossible to climb. Very frustrating!

Day 7 Didn't make much progress. Extremely depressing.	*Day 9* Reached the top at last! Tremendously exciting!
Day 8 Climb very difficult. A very hard day.	

1 The first day was **the easiest** because he didn't climb far.

2 The second day was ______________ because he climbed for eight hours.

3 The third day was ______________ because ____________________________.

4 The fourth day was ______________ because ____________________________.

5 The fifth day was ______________ because ____________________________.

6 The sixth day was ______________ because ____________________________.

7 The seventh day was ______________ because ____________________________.

8 The eighth day was ______________ because ____________________________.

9 The ninth day was ______________ because ____________________________.

EXERCISE 6

Complete the following television broadcast by putting the adjective in brackets into the correct form.

Welcome to the Paris Motor Show, where I've been looking at all (1) ________________________ (late) models, and there's no doubt in my mind that (2) ________________________ (impressive) car this year is this Metro 3.

As you can see, it's slightly (3) ________________________ (small) than many of the others on show, but inside it's (4) ________________________ (spacious) than it looks and, I have to admit, it's one of (5) ________________________ (comfortable) cars I've ever driven. The emphasis this year is on safety and economy. So, although it's not (6) ________________________ (fast) car here today, it's certainly (7) ________________________ (economical). It does (8) ________________________ (many) kilometres to the litre than any of the others. Changes in design have resulted in a (9) ________________________ (good), (10) ________________________ (efficient) braking system than in other models, and the introduction of power steering means it is (11) ________________________ (easy) to drive. In fact, tests have shown that this car is probably (12) ____________________ (safe) and (13) ____________________ (reliable) in the show.

The Metro 3 will cost around £9,500 and, from what I've seen of it, will definitely be (14) ____________________ (good) value for money in this price range.

6 ADVERBS

BIRD'S EYE BOX: Adverbs

I'm leaving **tomorrow**.	→	definite time (Exercise 1)
Think **before** you speak! We're nearly **there**. I can **never** remember his name.	→	position of adverbs of indefinite time, place and frequency (Exercises 2 and 9)
He **usually** gets home at 7.00.	→	adverbs of frequency (Exercises 3 and 9)
He spoke the language **fluently**.	→	adverbs of manner (Exercises 4, 5 and 9)
He got up **earlier** than usual. He began to walk **more quickly**.	→	comparative adverbs (Exercises 6, 7 and 9)
On the English side, Watson played **the most skilfully**. On the Irish side, O'Hara played **the best**.	→	superlative adverbs (Exercises 8 and 9)

EXERCISE 1

Make as many correct sentences as possible from boxes A, B *and* C. *Use the prepositions in box* B *only where necessary.*

Example: I'll have finished it | in two days' time.
by the end of the month.
by the morning.
by Tuesday.
by this afternoon.

A	B	C
He's starting I haven't seen him I'll pay you back It usually arrives He should have done it She left	in at since on by	a month ago. two days' time. the end of the month. the morning. Tuesday(s). last week. this afternoon. today.

EXERCISE 2

Decide which is the normal position in the sentence for the words in brackets. Then write the appropriate letter (a, b or c) in the box. Sometimes more than one position is possible. The first one has been done for you.

1 I've phoned several times, but (a) there (b) is (c) no answer. (still) [c]

2 Have you (a) been (b) to the Hebrides (c) ? (ever) [ ]

3 Ah, there it is! (a) I've been looking (b) for it (c) ! (everywhere) [ ]

4 Cigarette?
No thanks. I (a) have (b) put one (c) out. (just) [ ]

5 (a) wait (b) for me (c) . (outside) [ ]

6 (a) we don't (b) go out (c) on Saturday nights. (often) [ ]

7 Drink this and you (a) will (b) feel better (c) . (soon) [ ]

8 Like to have a look at the paper?
No thanks. I (a) have (b) seen it (c) . (already) [ ]

9 Excuse me. (a) is there (b) a garage (c) ? (near by) [ ]

10 Don't tell me the end of the film! I (a) haven't (b) seen it (c) ! (yet) [ ]

EXERCISE 3

Use the following notes and a suitable adverb from the box to complete the magazine article below. When there is more than one possibility, try to use as many different adverbs as possible. The first one has been done for you.

Robert Williams

1 interested in acting ever since he was a child

2 gets a part in the theatre now and then

3 is out of work sixty per cent of the time

4 helps in a friend's restaurant most of the time

5 is worried about money all the time

6 parents help him financially now and then

7 sees them only every two or three years

8 gets depressed from time to time

9 definitely wouldn't consider doing anything else

always	continually	ever	frequently	generally	hardly ever
never	occasionally	often	usually	rarely	sometimes

Life can be difficult for a young actor, as I found out when I visited Robert Williams at his home in Clapham. Robert (1) has **always** been interested in acting. If he's lucky, he (2) ______________________________, but he (3) ______________________________. To pay the rent he (4) ______________________________, but he (5) ______________________________. His (6) ______________________________, but as they live in New Zealand, he (7) ______________________________. He admits that he (8) ______________________________, but says he (9) ______________________________.

EXERCISE 4

Complete the following table.

	ADJECTIVE	ADVERB		ADJECTIVE	ADVERB
1	careful	carefully	6	good	
2	easy		7	bad	
3	hard		8	angry	
4	thorough		9	disapproving	
5	unfriendly		10	fast	

EXERCISE 5

Choose suitable adverbs to complete the following letter of reference. You should try to use as many different adverbs as possible. The first one has been done for you.

To Whom It May Concern

Miss Thomas has worked for this company for six years and has always been an (1) **extremely** reliable and co-operative employee. She is (2) ______________ well organised and does her work (3) ______________ and (4) ______________. She types (5) ______________ and writes shorthand (6) ______________. In addition, she speaks French (7) ______________ and can understand German (8) ______________ (9) ______________. Future employers will find that she always arrives (10) ____________ and works (11) ____________ (12) ____________.

We wish her every success in her future career.

D. Martin

Managing Director

EXERCISE 6

Complete the following advertisements. The first one has been done for you.

1 Headache? You want fast relief. Paradox works **faster** than any other tablet.

2 So your batteries last a long time, do they? Try Zenox batteries. They last even ____________.

3 If you think your washing powder gets your clothes thoroughly clean, then you haven't tried Dax. Dax will clean them ____________.

4 I never slept very well until I drank Nightcap. Now I sleep ____________ than ever before!

5 Money doesn't go very far nowadays, does it? So, shop at Savealot where your money goes ____________.

6 Do you wish your photocopier was quicker, more efficient? Then change to Speedman. Speedman copies ____________ and ____________ than most other copiers.

EXERCISE 7

Complete the following in an appropriate way. There is often more than one acceptable answer.

Example: I'm sorry. I don't understand. Could you **say it again more slowly**?
or Could you **speak less quickly**?

1 If you don't hurry up, I'll miss my train. Can't you ____________?

2 If you want to pass this exam, Thomas, you'll have to ____________.

3 Children, I know you're enjoying yourselves, but I've got a terrible headache. Please can you ____________________?

4 Daniel, there's a police car following us! Hadn't you better ____________________?

5 I can't understand what's happened to the team. They've been playing pretty badly all season and last night they ____________________ than usual!

6 I'm sorry, but this is a very bad line, and I can't hear you. Could you ____________________?

EXERCISE 8

*Use the word in brackets to complete the following. Use the article (**the**) only where necessary.*

Examples: He argued **most persuasively** (persuasive).
He argued **the most persuasively** of all the speakers (persuasive).

1 I know she thought about it (a) ____________________ (careful) before making a decision, and, taking everything into consideration, I think she acted (b) ____________________ (sensible).

2 Well, out of all the different machines to choose from, I'd say this model works (a) ____________________ (efficient), produces (b) ____________________ (good) copies and costs (c) ____________________ (little) to run.

3 I'm pleased to say all the ideas were received (a) ____________________ (favourable), but there's no doubt Mick's idea was received (b) ____________________ (enthusiastic), so that's the one we've chosen.

4 All the class has learned quite a lot, but Alfredo has definitely learned (a) ____________________ (more), which is not surprising, as he's always worked (b) ____________________ (hard).

5 Look, the man has written back to you (a) ____________________ (apologetic), explaining that there was a genuine mistake, so, under the circumstances, I think you're behaving (b) ____________________ (unreasonable).

EXERCISE 9

Read the following television interview. Then choose suitable adverbs to complete the discussion. There is often more than one acceptable answer. The first one has been done for you.

INTERVIEWER: My first guest this evening is the young British cyclist Ken Barclay. Ken has (1) **just** been chosen to ride in next year's *Tour de France*. Congratulations, Ken! How do you feel about it?

KEN: Thanks. Well, of course, I'm (2) ______________ pleased. I (3) ______________ expected to be selected.

INTERVIEWER: Which will be the most difficult part of the race for you?

KEN: Well, I'm not very good at climbing. I ride (4) ______________ on flat roads. So, I don't expect to do (5) ______________ in the mountains.

INTERVIEWER: You must have to do a lot of training, don't you?

KEN: Yes, of course. I train (6) ______________ for about five or six hours. But (7) ______________ I've been training even (8) ______________ than that. But I'm still not as good as I should be! You see, it's a very long race. You have to ride (9) ______________ than in most other races, and there are (10) ______________ any rest days, maybe only one or two. So, it's (11) ______________ tiring, too. You've got to be (12) ______________ fit.

INTERVIEWER: It's a dangerous sport, too, isn't it?

KEN: Oh, yes, (13) ______________! You have to ride so (14) ______________ to each other that it's very easy to fall. (15) ______________ the worst accident I've (16) ______________ had was breaking a finger, but some riders have been (17) ______________ injured. Some have even been killed.

INTERVIEWER: Well, Ken, the very best of luck in the *Tour*, and let's hope you finish the race (18) ______________!

7 QUANTIFIERS

BIRD'S EYE BOX: Quantifiers

We haven't got **much** time. How **many** people are coming?	→	**much/many** (Exercises 1 and 3)
		LARGE QUANTIFIERS
He showed **a great deal of** interest There's **plenty of** room. There are **a number of** problems.	→	**a great deal (of)/plenty (of)/a number (of)** (Exercises 2 and 3)
He's got **lots of/a lot of** ideas.	→	**a lot (of)/lots (of)** (Exercise 3)
		SMALL QUANTIFIERS
They had **a few** drinks. She's made **a little** progress.	→	**a few/a little** (Exercises 4, 5 and 8)
Few people have heard of him. She had **little** success.	→	**few/little** (Exercises 5 and 8)
There were **fewer** people than expected. He had **less** money than he thought.	→	**fewer/less** (Exercises 6 and 8)
		NEUTRAL QUANTIFIERS
Would you like **some** tea?	→	**some** in questions (Exercise 7)
I need **some** help. Have you made **any** plans yet?	→	**some/any** (Exercises 7 and 8)
He left **several** days later. She received **quite a few** offers.	→	**several/quite a few** (Exercise 8)

EXERCISE 1

Tom is talking to a friend about a party he went to. Complete the following with ***much*** *or* ***many****. The first one has been done for you.*

What was the party like ? Oh, not very good. There were too (1) <u>**many**</u> people there, so there wasn't (2) ______ room to dance or move about and talk to people. How (3) ______ people were there? About forty, I should think. Mind you, I didn't know (4) ______ of them and I'm not very good at talking to people I don't know. I didn't get there till late anyway, so, by the time I got there, there wasn't (5) ______ food left or (6) ______ drink either. I've been to one or two of her parties before, but not (7) ______. I don't think I'll go to another one. It wasn't (8) ______ fun.

EXERCISE 2

Complete the following with **a great deal (of), plenty (of)** *or* **a number (of)**. *Sometimes more than one answer is possible.*

Example: I don't know why you think she's lonely. She's got **plenty of** friends.

1 Being a primary school teacher, she must have __________ patience.

2 __________ people have asked me the same question. I'm afraid I really don't know the answer.

3 Come on, everyone. There's __________ food, so help yourselves!

4 I've complained about it __________ times, but they still haven't done anything about it.

5 There's no need to get any more petrol. There's __________ in the tank.

6 It's kind of you to offer, but there isn't really __________ work to do.

EXERCISE 3

Complete the following dialogue by choosing words from the box below. Frequently more than one answer is possible, but you should try and use each quantifier at least once. The first one has been done for you.

much   many   a lot (of)   lots (of)   a great deal (of) a number (of)   plenty (of)

DIRECTOR: Has there been (1) **much** response to the job advertisement?

MANAGER: Oh, yes. We've had (2) __________ applications. The only trouble is that not (3) __________ of them are really suitable. They've either got (4) __________ qualifications but not (5) __________ experience or vice versa. Take this girl, for example. She hasn't got (6) __________ qualifications, but she's had (7) __________ different jobs.

DIRECTOR: Still, sometimes experience is more important than qualifications. Anyway, we haven't got (8) ____________ time, so we'll have to make a decision soon. Have you any idea how (9) ____________ we'll need to interview?

MANAGER: Well, I've put (10) ____________ of them aside for you to look at, and then we can make a short list.

DIRECTOR: Fine. I've got (11) ____________ things to do this morning, but I should have (12) ____________ time this afternoon. So perhaps we can discuss it then.

MANAGER: That suits me.

EXERCISE 4

Complete the following weather forecast with **a few** *or* **a little***. The first one has been done for you.*

After a clear night, it will be a dry day in most places, though (1) **a few** areas will have (2) ____________ rain in the afternoon. In the south it will be rather dull with only (3) ____________ sunshine and the possibility of (4) ____________ showers later in the day. In the Midlands and East Anglia there may be (5) ____________ fog at first, but this should clear quickly, giving a bright day with temperatures (6) ____________ degrees above zero. The cold weather over Scotland is likely to continue for (7) ____________ more days, with (8) ____________ snow on high ground. However, milder weather is expected by the weekend.

EXERCISE 5

Complete the following conversations with **a few, few, a little** *or* **little***. The first one has been done for you.*

1 TOM: Oh, come on! Liverpool have very (a) **little** chance of winning! After all, they've lost nearly every match this season.

MICK: I'm not so sure. They've got (b) ____________ good players and, with (c) ____________ bit of luck, they might just beat Rangers.

2 DIRECTOR: A very successful meeting, don't you think?

CHAIRMAN: Very successful indeed. Just think, we've had (a) ____________ arguments, (b) ____________ disagreement and (c) ____________ objections. In fact, we've made quite a lot of progress.

3 STUDENT: You wanted (a) ______________ words with me, sir?

PRINCIPAL: Ah, yes, Patrick. Come in. It's about your work. Now, I know this exam is of (b) ______________ importance to you personally, but (c) ______________ of the students have complained about your behaviour in class. I would be grateful if you could make (d) ______________ more effort for the rest of the term.

EXERCISE 6

Read the following information about two cars. Then compare the saloon with the GT using **fewer** *and* **less**. *The first one has been done for you.*

The Saloon

1 2 doors
2 4 seats
3 Acceleration: 0–100 kms in 12 seconds
4 Petrol consumption: 20 kms to the litre
5 4 gears
6 Choice of colours: red, blue, grey
7 Extras: cigarette-lighter, radio

The GT

1 4 doors
2 6 seats
3 Acceleration: 0–100 kms in 7 seconds
4 Petrol consumption: 14 kms to the litre
5 5 gears
6 Choice of colours: red, black, silver, blue, yellow
7 Extras: cigarette-lighter, radio, cassette player, electric windows, air-conditioning

1 The saloon has **fewer** doors.
2 The saloon has ______________________________.
3 The saloon has ______________________________.
4 The saloon uses ______________________________.
5 The saloon has ______________________________.
6 There is ______________________________.
7 There are ______________________________.

EXERCISE 7

Some secretaries are talking at lunchtime. Complete the following sentences with **some** or **any**. The first one has been done for you.

1 'Thank goodness it's lunchtime! I'm starving! I didn't have **any** breakfast!'

2 'Have you got (a) ________ change, Barbara? I need (b) ________ for the coffee machine.'

3 'I'm going out. I've got (a) _______ shopping to do. We've got (b) _______ people coming for dinner and there isn't (c) _______ food in the house.'

4 'That smells nice, Pam. What is it?'
'It's home-made soup. Would you like to try _______?'

5 'Have _______ of you seen my lighter? I left it on my desk.'

6 'Oh, no! There isn't (a) _______ milk left!'
'Do you want (b) _______ of my powdered milk?'
'Thanks.'

EXERCISE 8

The actor Brian Amos is being interviewed. Complete the conversation by choosing words from the box below. Sometimes more than one answer is possible, but you should try to use each quantifier at least once. The first one has been done for you.

a few	few	a little	little	some	any	quite a few	several
fewer	less						

INTERVIEWER: Now, Brian, you've been voted Actor of the Year. How do you feel about that?

BRIAN: I'm delighted, of course, but I could name (1) **quite a few** actors who are better than I am. I've just had (2) ____________ more luck than they have. That's all.

INTERVIEWER: Is luck very important in the theatre, then?

BRIAN: Oh, definitely. You see, there are very (3) ____________ good parts, so it's very competitive.

INTERVIEWER: Did you find it difficult at first?

BRIAN: Yes, very. It was (4) ____________ months before I got my first job, and so I didn't have (5) ____________ money. Then I was lucky enough to get (6) ____________ small parts on television, but even then I earned very (7) ____________.

INTERVIEWER: But it must be easier now that you're well known.

BRIAN: Well, of course, I have (8) ____________ financial problems than I did before, but I still have to work just as hard. I mean, (9) ____________ people think actors have an easy life, only working in the evenings. Well, that's quite wrong. During the day we have to rehearse new plays or look for more work, so we probably have (10) ______________ free time than most people.

INTERVIEWER: And have you got (11) ______________ idea what you'll do next?

BRIAN: Well, there are (12) ______________ things I'm interested in doing. I've had (13) ______________ offers from film directors and producers, but I haven't made (14) ______________ definite plans yet.

INTERVIEWER: Brian Amos, thank you for talking to me.

8 MODALS

BIRD'S EYE BOX: Modals

Shall I do it for you?	→	**shall, will, could** (offers, requests, suggestions, willingness) (Exercises 1 and 11)
I'd rather watch the film than the football match.	→	**would like to/prefer to/sooner/ rather** (preferences) (Exercises 2 and 11)
You'**d better** go home.	→	**had better, should, ought to** (advice/moral obligation) (Exercises 3 and 11)
Can you drive?	→	**can, could, may, might** (ability, permission, possibility) (Exercises 4, 5 and 11)
He **wasn't able to** be there.	→	**be able to, be allowed to** (ability, permission) (Exercises 5 and 11)
You **must** work harder!	→	**must, have to** (obligation) (Exercises 6 and 11)
You **needn't** do it now.	→	**mustn't, needn't, don't have to** (negative obligation/absence of obligation) (Exercises 7 and 11)
You **can't have** forgotten already!	→	**must, must have, can't, can't have** (logical conclusion) (Exercises 8 and 11)
Didn't he **use to** live near you?	→	**used to** (past habit) (Exercises 9, 10 and 11)
He **would** think about it for hours before making a decision.	→	**would** (past habit) (Exercise 10)

EXERCISE 1

Complete the following short dialogues by choosing from the boxes below. You should make combinations from A + B + D *or* C + D. *The first one has been done for you.*

A	B	C	D
Shall Will Could	I you we	I'll	have a look at it stay for lunch put the kettle on have another piece go to the cinema get them have the salt eat out get some stamps show you how to use it

1 'Let's have a cup of tea.'
'Good idea. **Shall I put the kettle on?'**

2 '________________________, please?'
'Here you are. Do you want the pepper as well?'

3 'David, there's something wrong with the iron.'
'All right. ________________________ later.'

4 '________________________ this evening?'
'That's a good idea. What's on?'

5 '________________________?'
'I'd love to, but I really can't. I have to be home by 1.00.'

6 'I'm just going down to the Post Office.'
'Oh, ________________________ for me, please?'

7 'This is a lovely cake, Jean. Did you make it yourself?'
'Yes, I did. ________________________?'

8 'I really can't work this telex machine!'
'It's easy. ________________________?'

9 '________________________ tonight for a change?'
'No, I think I'd prefer to eat at home.'

10 'Oh, dear! I've left my glasses upstairs.'
'Don't move. ________________________ for you.'

EXERCISE 2

Complete the following short dialogues by putting the words provided into the correct form and choosing a suitable verb to follow. Read each dialogue carefully as you will sometimes need to use negatives. The first one has been done for you.

1 like sooner

'We're going shopping this afternoon. (a) **Would** you **like to come** with us?'

'It's nice of you to ask me, but I (b) ______________ at home if you don't mind. I'm quite tired.'

2 like rather prefer

'What shall I get Harry for his birthday? Do you think he (a) ______________ something to wear or (b) ______________ he ______________ money?'

'Well, I expect he (c) ______________ his own clothes, so I'd give him money.'

3 rather sooner

'Shall we go to France again this year or (a) ______________ you ______________ somewhere else?'

'Well, I (b) ______________ anywhere too hot. I don't like too much sun.'

4 prefer sooner like

'You look very tired, dear. (a) ______________ you ______________ instead of going out for a meal?'

'No, I (b) ______________, but I (c) ______________ a rest before we go.'

5 like rather

'Honestly, I know she earns a lot of money, but look how hard she works! I (a) ______________ her job!'

'Nor would I. I (b) ______________ less money and have more free time, wouldn't you?'

6 prefer like

'Well, we can only advise you, Mr Shelley. It's really your decision.'

'Yes, I know, but I (a) ______________ a decision immediately. I (b) ______________ a few days to think about it.'

EXERCISE 3

Which of the following sentences can take **had better (not)** *and which must take* **should(n't)** *or* **ought(n't) to**? *Complete the following, using* **had better (not)** *where possible.*

Examples: Alison doesn't feel very well, **I'd better** take her home.

I think the Government **should** spend more on education. Don't you?

1 We ____________ leave quite early in the morning. The traffic's terrible.

2 You ____________ give it to me. I might lose it. Give it to Edward.

3 Do you think mothers with very young children ____________ go out to work?

4 ____________ you ____________ tell him before he finds out?

5 The question we want to discuss is '____________ violent films be shown on television?'

6 In my opinion, the police already have enough power. They ____________ be given any more.

7 We ____________ make too much noise or the neighbours might complain.

8 I think I ____________ take an umbrella. It looks like rain.

9 ____________ you ____________ check the times of the train before we leave?

10 You ____________ be so impatient. It's not my fault if I don't understand!

EXERCISE 4

Complete the following, using **can('t), could(n't), may (not)** *or* **might (not)** *and choosing a suitable verb from the box below. Do not use any verb more than once. There is sometimes more than one acceptable answer. The first one has been done for you.*

come go have leave read take turn understand use

1 Honestly, he spoke so fast I **couldn't understand** a word he said!

2 ________ we ________ our cases here while we have lunch?

3 I'd take a coat with you. It ________ cold later.

4 ________ I ________ your phone? Ours is out of order.

5 I'd like to go to Sally's party, but I ________ time.

6 If you don't want to drive, you ________ always ________ by train.

7 Tom's a very good pianist, even though he ________ a note of music!

8 The House of Commons was interesting, but we ________ photos, which was a pity.

EXERCISE 5

Complete the following news items by choosing from boxes A or B. There is often more than one acceptable answer. The first one has been done for you.

A

can can't
could couldn't
might might not
may may not

B

will be won't be
is isn't are aren't
was wasn't were weren't
\+ allowed to / able to

1

Mrs Hilda Barker, who lost her eyesight five years ago (a) **can** now see again, thanks to surgeons at Moorfields Eye Hospital. Mrs Barker said, 'I (b) ________ ________ tell you how wonderful it was when I opened my eyes and I (c) ________ ________ see!' A hospital spokesman said, 'There is always the chance that she (d) ________ ________ lose her sight again, but we doubt it.' Mrs Barker hopes she (e) ________ leave hospital in two weeks' time.

2

John Barratt, M. P., is looking into the case of a Vietnamese refugee who (a) ________________ enter the country because his papers were not in order. 'The poor man (b) ________________ speak a word of English,' said Mr Barratt, 'so he (c) ________________ understand what was happening. He's obviously very worried that the Government (d) ________________ let him stay here. I hope I (e) ________________ do something for him, but it (f) ________________ take several weeks.'

3

Two schoolgirls, who were sent home for wearing make-up, (a) ________________ miss their university entrance examinations if they (b) ________________ return to school next week. 'If the girls (c) ________________ take these exams,' complained one parent, 'they (d) ________________ go to university. I know they broke the school rules, but the headmaster is being unreasonable.' The headmaster, James Craig, said, 'The girls knew they (e) ________________ wear make-up, but they did. However, if they are prepared to apologise, I (f) ________________ consider letting them return.'

EXERCISE 6

Complete the following sentences by choosing the correct words (a or b) and write the appropriate letter in the box. Sometimes both answers are possible.

Example: As he's the managing director, the <u>a/b</u> attend a lot of meetings.
(a) must (b) has to [b]

1 It's a really good film. You ______________ go and see it.
(a) must (b) have to ☐

2 Remind me to go to the bank at lunchtime. I ______________ cash a cheque.
(a) must (b) have to ☐

3 Richard's long-sighted. He ______________ wear glasses for reading.
(a) must (b) has to ☐

4 You can't go straight on. It's a one-way street. You ______________ go round the market square.
(a) must (b) have to ☐

5 I'm not going out for lunch. I've got some work I ______________ finish.
(a) must (b) have to ☐

6 I really ______________ wash my hair tonight. It's filthy!
(a) must (b) have to ☐

7 It's my mother's birthday on Friday. I ______________ remember to get her a card.
(a) must (b) have to ☐

8 Your father's already gone to bed. He ______________ go to work tomorrow.
(a) must (b) has to ☐

EXERCISE 7

Read the following and then complete the spaces by choosing from boxes A *and* B. *Each phrase in box* B *should be used twice. The first one has been done for you.*

A
mustn't
needn't
don't have to

B	
do it	get up yet
drive so fast	say it again
eat it	tell the others

1 You **mustn't tell the others**. It's confidential.

2 You ______________________________. You're not well enough.

3 You ______________________________. I heard you the first time!

4 You ______________________________. I've already told them.

5 You ______________________________ if it's poisonous.

6 You ______________________________. It's not polite!

7 You ______________________________. We've got plenty of time.

8 You ______________________________. It's only 5.00 a.m.

9 You ________________________________ if it's dangerous.

10 You ________________________________ if you don't like it.

11 You ________________________________. There's a thirty m.p.h. speed limit.

12 You ________________________________ if you don't want to.

EXERCISE 8

Complete the following with **must, can't, must have** *or* **can't have** *and the correct form of the verb in brackets. The first one has been done for you.*

1 'Bill (a) can't (be) serious about giving up his job, surely?'
'I think he is.'
'Well, in that case, he (b) ________________________ (be) mad!'

2 'Oh, you (a) ________________________ (know) who I mean! She's terribly famous and she's made lots of films. You (b) ________________________ (see) her!'

3 'There's no answer. They (a) ________________________ (be) in.'
'Don't be silly. They (b) ________________________ (go) out. They're expecting us. They (c) ________________________ (be) in the garden.'

4 'Have the police got any idea how the man got in?'
'Well, they say he (a) ________________________ (climb) through a window, as they were all closed. So they think he (b) ________________________ (have) a master key.'

5 'That's Barbara over there, isn't it?'
'No, it (a) ________________________ (be). That girl's much too fat.'
'It is Barbara, you know.'
'Well, she (b) ________________________ (put) on a lot of weight, then!'

6 'My keys (a) ________________________ (be) here somewhere. I (b) ________________________ (lose) them.'
'You (c) ________________________ (have) some idea where you put them, surely?'

EXERCISE 9

Amy Cathcart has lived in the same street for fifty years. What did life use to be like? Read what she says and then complete the exercise below, using **used to** *or* **didn't use to**. *The first one has been done for you.*

Well, (1) it's not as friendly as in the old days, with (2) neighbours calling in on each other. (3) People don't leave their doors open any more. Perhaps it's because (4) there's more crime nowadays. I don't know. (5) The traffic's much worse, too, so (6) children can't play in the street any more. It's too dangerous. I don't know where they go instead, as (7) most mothers go out to work nowadays. Of course, (8) mothers always stayed at home when I was young. In some ways life's easier nowadays, but I miss the community feeling we used to have.

1 **It used to be more friendly.**
2 ______________.
3 ______________.
4 ______________.
5 ______________.
6 ______________.
7 ______________.
8 ______________.

EXERCISE 10

Which of the following sentences can take **would** *and which must take* **used to**? *Complete the following, using* **would** *wherever possible, even though* **used to** *is also correct.*

Examples: She **used to** be a concert pianist.

She **would** practise every day for hours.

1 Bob was such an enthusiastic photographer that he ______________ spend all day trying to get the right photo.

2 Before he was transferred, Gary North ______________ play for Leeds.

3 The two friends had very strong opinions and ______________ argue passionately about anything they believed in.

4 On her way to work, Hilary ______________ stop at the newsagent's and buy a paper to read on the train.

5 Before they opened the by-pass, the traffic ______________ be much worse in the city centre.

6 In winter, the old men ______________ sit in the library where it was warm.

7 I ______________ like her before she got promotion and became very self-important.

8 Alan didn't get on with his mother-in-law. So, whenever she came to visit, he ______________ find an excuse to go out.

EXERCISE 11

Complete the following pieces of conversation, heard at a party, with a suitable modal verb. Sometimes there may be more than one acceptable answer. The first one has been done for you.

'Are you going already?'

'Yes, we (1) **have to** take the babysitter home.'

(2) '__________ I get your coats for you?'

'Another glass of wine, Harry?'

'No, thanks. I (3) __________ have a beer this time.'

'Harry, you (4) __________ drink too much or you (5) __________ drive home!'

'Who's that man over there, talking to Peter?'

'Oh, I (6) __________ remember his name, but I think he (7) __________ work with Sheila before she changed her job.'

'You (8) __________ be Sheila's sister! You look just like her!'

'I thought Tom was coming to the party.'

'Oh, he phoned earlier to say he (9) __________ be late.'

'You (10) __________ try one of these sandwiches, Terry. They're awfully nice.'

(11) '__________ you __________ dance, Catherine?'

'Not really, if you don't mind. I (12) __________ sit here and talk.'

'It's getting awfully late, Derek. We (13) __________ go home.'

'Oh, we (14) __________ leave yet. Tomorrow's Saturday.'

(15) '__________ I open a window, Sheila? It's awfully hot in here.'

'Yes, of course. (16) __________ you manage, or (17) __________ I do it for you?'

'I (18) __________ give you a lift home if you like, Mary.'

'If you (19) __________ drop me off at the end of my road, I'd be very grateful.'

'Lovely party, Sheila. Thanks for inviting us.'

'Well, I was glad you (20) __________ come.'

9 TENSES

BIRD'S EYE BOX: Tenses

What **are** you doing? He **didn't** say anything. It**'s** made of solid gold. How long **have** you been here?	→	**be, do, have** as auxiliaries (Exercise 1)
He **comes** from Hull, but he**'s studying** electronics in London.	→	present simple, present continuous (Exercises 2, 8, 9 and 10)
Do what I tell you and **don't argue**!	→	imperative (Exercises 3, 8 and 10)
He **cut** himself while he **was shaving**. She still **hasn't come**, and we**'ve been waiting** for an hour! Everyone knew he**'d lost** his job because he**'d been cheating** the company.	→	past simple, past continuous, present perfect simple, present perfect continuous, past perfect simple, past perfect continuous (Exercises 4, 5, 8, 9 and 10)
I'll see you later. What **are** you **going to do**? They**'re leaving** in the morning. The plane **lands** at 4.30.	→	**will, going to**: present continuous as a future, present simple as a future (Exercises 6, 8, 9 and 10)
We**'ll be having** dinner at 7.30, but we**'ll have finished** by 8.00. They**'ll have been going** out together for three years by the end of July.	→	future continuous, future perfect, future perfect continuous (Exercises 7 and 9)
The Queen **is to visit** Nepal in the autumn.	→	**be to** (Exercise 9)

EXERCISE 1

Complete the following letter with the correct form of **be, do** *or* **have**. *Read the letter carefully before you start, as you will sometimes need to use negatives. The first one has been done for you.*

Dear Graham,

I'm sorry to say that we (1) **are** having a disastrous holiday! To start with, the plane (2) ____________ delayed for six hours, so we (3) ____________ arrive until 3.00 a.m. Fortunately, the courier (4) ____________ still waiting to meet us, but when we got to the hotel, we found they (5) ____________ double-booked our room! So now we (6) ____________ staying in another hotel, which, believe it or not, (7) ____________ still being built! This means we (8) ____________ woken up every morning by the workmen. Why (9) ____________ it always happen to us?! It's not a very good hotel, either. The shower (10) ____________ work, and yesterday, when we (11) ____________ getting ready for dinner, the water supply (12) ____________ cut off. I complained to the manager, but he (13) ____________ seem very interested, and, of course, he (14) ____________ done anything about it yet. He has a typical 'let's wait until tomorrow' attitude. (15) ____________ you know what I mean?

The weather (16) ____________ been pretty awful since we got here. Last Saturday we took a train to the capital. (17) ____________ you ever been there? There's nothing much to see, and when we arrived we found Angela (18) ____________ forgotten the traveller's cheques, so we (19) ____________ speak to each other for the rest of the day! It (20) ____________ raining again this morning, and, as there's nothing else to do, I (21) ____________ writing a few letters. Also, we (22) ____________ both had bad stomachs for the last couple of days, so we (23) ____________ want to go too far from the hotel!

By the way, (24) ____________ you remember to video the Cup Final for me last weekend? It (25) ____________ matter if you forgot. I hear Sheffield City lost, which (26) ____________ surprise me, as they (27) ____________ been playing very badly recently.

Well, we'll see you in another week and, quite honestly, we won't be sorry to come home. With the food, the weather and the hotel, I (28) ______________ think we'll (29) ______________ coming here again!

Regards,
Derek

EXERCISE 2

Complete the following dialogues by putting the verbs in brackets into the correct form. Use only the present continuous or the present simple. Where there is also an adverb in the brackets, decide the correct position in the sentence. The first one has been done for you.

1 A: How (a) do you work (work) this photocopier? I (b) ______________ (think) I (c) ______________ (do) something wrong.

B: Yes, you (d) ______________ (press) the wrong button. That one (e) ______________ (enlarge) the copies. You (f) ______________ (need) to press this one.

A: Oh, yes. It (g) ______________ (work) properly now. Thanks.

2 A: I (a) ______________ (see) the price of petrol (b) ______________ (go) up again.

B: Yes, I (c) ______________ (know). I (d) ______________ (seriously consider) selling the car. It's so expensive, and we (e) ______________ (not often use) it.

A: What (f) ______________ your wife ______________ (think) of that idea?

B: She (g) ______________ (agree) with me. She (h) ______________ (not like) driving anyway.

3 A: Good-morning. Is Mr Cranshaw in?

B: Yes, he is, but he (a) ______________ (see) someone at the moment. (b) he ______________ (expect) you?

A: Yes, I (c) ______________ (have) an appointment with him at 10.30. My name's Phillips.

B: Ah, yes, Mr Phillips. I'm afraid we (d) ______________ (run) a little late this morning, but I (e) ______________ (not expect) Mr Cranshaw will be long, if you (f) ______________ (not mind) waiting.

4 A: Why (a) ______________ we ______________ (wait)?
B: John isn't here yet. I (b) ______________ (expect) he (c) ______________ (have) trouble with his car again.
A: Oh! That car (d) ______________ (always go) wrong! Well, I (e) ______________ (not wait) any longer. I (f) ______________ (not want) to miss the start of the match. (g) ______________ you ______________ (come) with me, or not?

5 A: What (a) ______________ you ______________ (make), Pamela? It (b) ______________ (smell) really nice.
B: Well, I (c) ______________ (try) a recipe my mother-in-law gave me. It (d) ______________ (sound) really easy. You (e) ______________ (cut) up the meat and vegetables and then you (f) ______________ (just add) a few herbs. When she (g) ______________ (make) it, it (h) ______________ (taste) really delicious. But I'm not sure about this. It (i) ______________ (not look) quite right.

6 A: What (a) ______________ you ______________ (think) of that new girl, Jacqueline?
B: Well, frankly, I (b) ______________ (find) her terribly annoying. She (c) ______________ (always make) silly remarks and she (d) ______________ (never listen) to anything you say.
A: I (e) ______________ (know) what you (f) ______________ (mean), but I (g) ______________ (feel) a bit sorry for her, actually. I (h) ______________ (think) she (i) ______________ (try) to hide her shyness by being funny, but she (j) ______________ (only succeed) in getting on everyone's nerves!

EXERCISE 3

Complete the following by selecting from the boxes below. Use the ideas in box C or make combinations from A + C or B + C. The first one has been done for you.

A	C
Do Do not Don't	tell me about it forget your key help yourselves go somewhere else turn off the electricity supply go for a walk say I'm out disturb

B
Let's

1 OK, everyone. There's plenty to eat and drink, so **do help yourselves**!

2 I'm tired of staying indoors. I need some fresh air. ____________.

3 I'll be in bed when you come home, so ____________.

4 It sounds terribly exciting! ____________!

5 Examination in progress. ____________.

6 ____________ before repairing the machine.

7 I'm busy, so if anyone phones, please ____________.

8 I'm fed up with going to discos! ____________ for a change!

EXERCISE 4

How many meaningful and grammatically correct sentences can you make by combining the ideas in boxes A, B and C?

Example: **They were driving home when the car broke down.**

A	B	C
They were driving home He didn't know what to do He's been working here I haven't seen him We'd already left The police arrived She was keeping watch We'd been enjoying ourselves	when while since before as soon as just as by the time	the trouble started. you've been away. they began arguing. he was counting the money. he left school. the car broke down. it started to rain.

EXERCISE 5

A woman has been accused of shop-lifting. Complete the following extract from her trial by putting the verbs in brackets into the correct form. The first one has been done for you.

PROSECUTION: Mr Williams, you (1) <u>were</u> (be) the security officer on duty at Malgo Department Store on July 28th. Please tell the court what (2) ____________ (happen) that afternoon.

WILLIAMS: Yes, sir. I (3) ____________ (be) particularly interested in the cosmetics department, because the company (4) ____________ (lose) a lot of money through shop-lifting earlier in the year. So, I (5) ____________ (watch) the customers on the security screen when I (6) ____________ (notice) a woman behaving rather suspiciously.

PROSECUTION: What exactly (7) ____________ she ____________ (do)?

WILLIAMS: Well, she (8) ____________ (seem) rather nervous and she (9) ____________ (keep) looking round as if she (10) ____________ (want) to make sure that no one (11) ____________ (watch) her.

PROSECUTION: (12) ____________ you ever ____________ (see) the woman before that afternoon?

WILLIAMS: No, sir. She (13) ____________ (not be) one of our regular customers.

PROSECUTION: I see. Please go on.

WILLIAMS: Well, then she suddenly (14) ____________ (pick) up a bottle of perfume and (15) ____________ (put) it in her shopping bag.

PROSECUTION: And she (16) ____________ (not pay) for the perfume, I presume?

WILLIAMS: No, sir. And then she (17) ____________ (leave) the store.

PROSECUTION: So what (18) ____________ you ____________ (do)?

WILLIAMS: I (19) ____________ (follow) her and (20) ____________ (ask) her to return to the manager's office. When she (21) ____________ (empty) her bag, we (22) ____________ (find) that she (23) ____________ (take) a lipstick and some mascara as well.

PROSECUTION: And she (24) ____________ (not pay) for any of them?

WILLIAMS: No, sir.

PROSECUTION: Mr Williams, how long (25) ____________ you ____________ (work) at Malgo Department Store?

WILLIAMS: For about three years, sir.

PROSECUTION: And (26) ______________ you ______________ (catch) many shop-lifters in that time?

WILLIAMS: Quite a few, sir. Shop-lifting is a problem in any big store.

PROSECUTION: Quite. So you always know when someone is about to take goods without paying?

WILLIAMS: Not always, sir. But over the years I (27) ______________ (learn) to recognise the signals.

PROSECUTION: Thank you, Mr Williams. That is all.

EXERCISE 6

Choose the best words (a, b, c or d) to complete the sentence and write the appropriate letter in the box. Sometimes more than one option is acceptable.

Example: Right. I ______________ you up at 7.30, if that's convenient.
(a) am going to pick (b) am picking (c) will pick (d) pick [c]

1 What ______________ to Sandra's party on Saturday?
(a) are you going to wear (b) are you wearing (c) will you wear
(d) do you wear [ ]

2 We'd better hurry up. The train ______________ in half an hour.
(a) is going to leave (b) is leaving (c) will leave (d) leaves [ ]

3 He ______________ sociology at university in the autumn.
(a) is going to study (b) is studying (c) will study (d) studies [ ]

4 I'm just going to the bank. I ______________ long.
(a) am not going to be (b) am not being (c) won't be (d) don't be [ ]

5 I've got an appointment with the dentist tomorrow. I expect he ______________ something wrong. He always does!
(a) is going to find (b) is finding (c) will find (d) finds [ ]

6 There's a good film on television tonight. What time ______________?
(a) is it going to start (b) is it starting (c) will it start
(d) does it start [ ]

7 We ______________ to the States to spend Christmas with our son.
(a) are going to fly (b) are flying (c) will fly (d) fly [ ]

8 You've got plenty of time. The plane ______________ off until 4.30.
(a) isn't going to take (b) isn't taking (c) won't take
(d) doesn't take [ ]

9 That really makes me angry! This time I ______________ to him about it!
(a) am going to speak (b) am speaking (c) will speak (d) speak ☐

10 If you give me that letter now, I ______________ it on my way home.
(a) am going to post (b) am posting (c) will post (d) post ☐

EXERCISE 7

Jenny and Peter are going to drive from London to Brussels next weekend. Look at the map and their itinerary and then complete the exercise below. Use the **will be doing, will have done** *or* **will have been doing** *forms of the verbs in brackets in your answers. The first one has been done for you.*

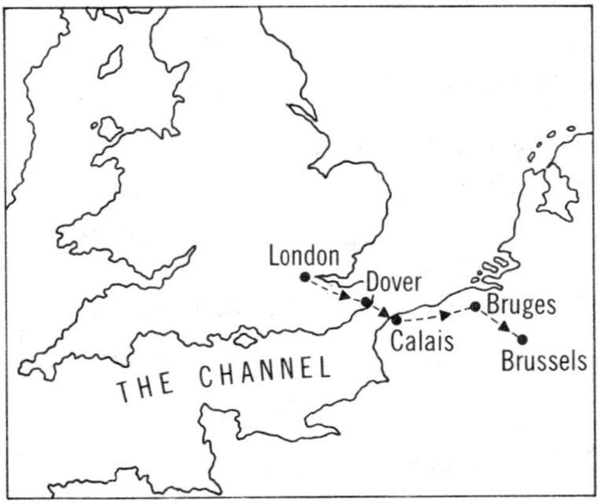

0730	Leave London
0930	Arrive in Dover
1030	Cross the Channel
1200	Arrive in Calais Stop for lunch
1330	Leave Calais
1530	Get to Bruges
1630	Reach Brussels

1 By 0800 **they'll have left London** (leave).
2 At 0830 ______________________________ (drive).
3 By 1000 ______________________________ (arrive).
4 By lunchtime ______________________________ (cross).
5 At 1300 ______________________________ (have lunch).
6 At 1500 ______________________________ (drive).
7 By 1545 ______________________________ (get to).
8 By 1700 ______________________________ (reach).
9 By the time they reach Brussels ______________ (travel) for nine hours.

EXERCISE 8

Complete the following letter by putting the verbs in brackets into the correct form. Occasionally there is more than one possible answer. The first one has been done for you.

Dear Debbie,

Thanks very much for your letter, which (1) **arrived** (arrive) more than six weeks ago! I (2) ____________ (mean) to reply to it for ages, but I just (3) ____________ (not have) time.

As you (4) ____________ (know), I (5) ____________ (start) a new job at the beginning of the month and I (6) ____________ (work) incredibly hard ever since. It's quite interesting, and I (7) ____________ (like) my new boss, but I (8) ____________ (not finish) until six o'clock and when I (9) ____________ (get) home, I'm too tired to do anything! Anyway, I (10) ____________ (tell) you all about it another time.

I (11) ____________ (take) a week's holiday very soon and I (12) ____________ (think) of coming to London the weekend after next. My sister (13) ____________ (invite) me to stay with her for a few days because her husband (14) ____________ (go) to France on business for a week. (15) ____________ you ____________ (make) any plans for that weekend? If not, (16) ____________ (meet) for lunch on the Saturday or Sunday. It's ages since I last (17) ____________ (see) you and I (18) ____________ (have) lots to tell you. Anyway, I (19) ____________ (phone) you during the week to see if you're free.

With love,

Alison

P.S. (20) ____________ (give) my regards to Chris.

EXERCISE 9

Read the following items from the **Barston Gazette**, *a local newspaper. Then complete the articles by putting the verbs in brackets into the correct form. Occasionally there is more than one possible answer. The first one has been done for you.*

1

Schoolboy Saved from River

Local schoolboy Brian Walker (a) **is recovering** (recover) in hospital after falling into the River Bar. Mr Paul Bates, who (b) ________________ (take) his dog for a walk at the time, (c) ________________ (jump) into the water and (d) ________________ (pull) the boy to safety. Brian (e) ________________ (play) on the river bank when the accident (f) ________________ (happen).

2

Lorries Anger Residents

Residents of Beechwood Avenue (a) ________________ (protest) to the council about the number of lorries using the road. 'They (b) ________________ (drive) down our road to avoid going through the High Street,' (c) ________________ (complain) one resident. 'But they (d) ________________ (make) so much noise that I (e) ________________ (not be able) to sleep for weeks. And they (f) ________________ (always break) the speed limit! One day there (g) ________________ (be) a serious accident, if the council (h) ________________ (not stop) them.'

3

Give Generously on Saturday!

Next Saturday, Friends of Barston Hospital (a) ________________________ (collect) money in the High Street to buy more equipment for the hospital. 'We (b) ________________________ (hope) that by the end of the day we (c) ________________________ (raise) at least £800,' (d) ________________________ (say) the organiser. 'We (e) ________________________ (need) a new incubator for premature babies and this money (f) ________________________ (help) us buy one.' At the moment the Friends (g) ________________________ (look) for volunteers to help on Saturday.

4

Cottage Destroyed by Fire

Police (a) ________________________ (think) that children accidentally (b) ________________________ (start) the fire that (c) ________________________ (burn) down an empty cottage in Woodend Lane last Sunday. Neighbours (d) ________________________ (call) the fire brigade, but, by the time they (e) ________________________ (arrive), the roof (f) ________________________ (fall) in. Workmen (g) ________________________ (now demolish) the remains of the cottage.

5

Fred Dies at 101

Barston's oldest inhabitant, Fred Whyte, (a) ________________________ (die) at the age of 101. Fred (b) ________________________ (live) in Barston since

1924 and (c) ______________________ (teach) at the local primary school until he (d) ________________ _______ (retire) in 1950. His funeral (e) ___________ ___________ (take) place next Friday.

6

Novelist to Open Library

The popular novelist Barbara Bartlett (a) _________ ______________ (open) the new extension to Barston library next Wednesday afternoon. Miss Bartlett, who (b) ______________________ (write) more than twenty best-selling novels, (c) ________________ _______ (sign) copies of her latest book from three to four o'clock.

EXERCISE 10

Read the following story about a man who found a leak (a small hole in a water-pipe) in his bathroom. Then complete the story by putting the verbs in brackets into the correct form. The first one has been done for you.

Richard Barnes (1) **had just come** (just come) home from work when he (2) ________________________________ (find) a leak in the bathroom. Water (3) ________________________________ (drip) from the ceiling for some time, and there (4) ________________________________ (be) a large pool of water on the floor. As soon as he (5) ______________________________ (see) the leak, he (6) ______________________________ (call) the plumber. The plumber's wife (7) ______________________________ (answer). 'I'm afraid he (8) ______________________________ (go) out an hour ago and he (9) ______________________________ (not come) back yet. I (10) _______ ______________________ (tell) him to phone you when he (11) _________ ______________________ (come) in. I (12) ________________________ ________ (not expect) he (13) ______________________________ (be) long.'

Richard (14) ______________________ (hang) up and (15) ______________________ (sit) down to wait. Two hours later the phone (16) ______________________ (ring).

'This is the plumber. I (17) ______________________ (believe) you (18) ______________________ (call) earlier.'

'Where on earth (19) ______________________ you ______________________ (be)?' (20) ______________________ (demand) Richard angrily. 'I (21) ______________________ (wait) for two hours! What (22) ______________________ you ______________________ (do) all this time?'

'I'm terribly sorry, sir,' the plumber (23) ______________________ (answer) nervously. 'I (24) ______________________ (have) a breakdown while I (25) ______________________ (drive) along the motorway. I (26) ______________________ (only just get) home. I (27) ______________________ (not even have) my dinner yet. My wife (28) ______________________ (get) it now.'

'Well, I'm sorry about your breakdown,' (29) ______________________ (say) Richard in a more friendly voice. 'But (30) ______________________ you ______________________ (repair) my leak tonight or not?'

'(31) ______________________ (not worry), sir,' (32) ______________________ (reply) the plumber. 'I (33) ______________________ (have) my dinner and then I (34) ______________________ (come) straight round.'

Richard (35) ______________________ (put) down the receiver and (36) ______________________ (go) back into the bathroom. The water (37) ______________________ (still drip) slowly into the bowl he (38) ______________________ (put) under the leak. He (39) ______________________ (empty) the bowl again and then (40) ______________________ (sit) down to wait. Two hours later he (41) ______________________ (pick) up the receiver again. Just as he (42) ______________________ (dial) the number, the doorbell (43) ______________________ (ring).

'I'm terribly sorry, sir,' (44) ______________________ (say) a small, dark-haired man apologetically. 'I (45) ______________________ (think) I (46) ______________________ (have) to get a new car!'

10 UNREAL PAST

BIRD'S EYE BOX: Unreal past

It's time we **left**.	→	**it's (high) time** (Exercise 1)
I'd rather/sooner you **told** him yourself.	→	**would rather/sooner** (Exercise 2)
I **wish** I **had** more time. **If only** I **hadn't done** it.	→	**wish/if only** (Exercise 3)
Suppose someone **saw** you? **Suppose** someone **had seen** you?	→	**suppose** (Exercise 4)
You talk **as if/as though** you **didn't like** him. She acts **as if/as though I'd done** something awful!	→	**as if/as though** (Exercise 5)

EXERCISE 1

Mary Adams is talking to her son, Gerry. Read the following and then complete the exercise below by changing the clause or sentence after each number (1, 2, etc.) so that it begins with **It's time** *or* **It's high time**. *The first one has been done for you.*

Are you still in bed, Gerry? It's 11.30 and (1) you still haven't got up yet! What are you? A child? (2) You should grow up! It's ridiculous at your age. I don't understand you at all! (3) You don't do any work. (4) You don't earn any money. You can't expect your father to support you all your life! (5) You should find a job! We're not made of money, you know. (6) You should start to consider your father and me!

1 **It's time you got up.**

2 It's high time ______.

3 It's ______.

4 ______.

5 ______.

6 ______.

EXERCISE 2

Use the following sentences to complete the letter below. Begin each phrase with ***I'd rather*** *or* ***I'd sooner****. The first one has been done for you.*

1 I don't want anyone else to know.

2 Please don't say anything to anyone.

3 Think about it carefully.

4 Please be honest and tell me.

5 Do what you think is right.

6 Please don't phone me at work.

MINISTRY OF DEFENCE

Memorandum

To: Major Reginald Armstrong

From: Sir Frederick Halt

Date: 2 April 19—

Just a note to remind you of our recent conversation and the offer I made you. (1) **I'd rather no one knew** about it for the time being. It's not exactly top secret, but you know what the newspapers are like. So, (2) ____________________ for the moment, not even your wife. Please don't feel you have to make a decision immediately. (3) ____________________ first of all. And don't feel you have to accept just because we're old friends. If you're not interested (4) ____________________. I've always respected your strength of character, Reggie, so (5) ____________________.

Incidentally, (6) ____________________. You never know who might be listening. Call me at home when you're ready.

Freddie

EXERCISE 3

Paul's at an informal party. Use the following information to complete Paul's thoughts. Begin each sentence with **I wish** *or* **If only**. *The first one has been done.*

1 He doesn't know anyone.

2 He's shy.

3 He's sorry he came to the party.

4 He feels nervous.

5 He's sorry he didn't stay at home.

6 He's sorry he's put on a suit.

7 He doesn't have much self-confidence.

8 He can't dance.

EXERCISE 4

Read the following television announcement and then complete the dialogue below. Begin each phrase with **Suppose**. *The first one has been done for you.*

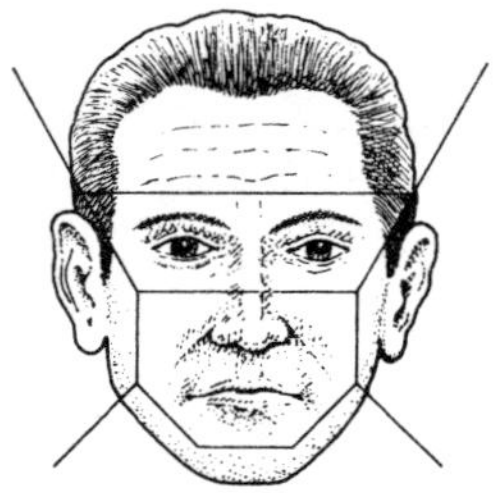

The police have issued this photofit picture of the man they wish to question about the recent attacks in Brentford. (1) Do you recognise this man? (2) Do you know who he is? (3) Is he a friend of yours? (4) Were you in the area when the attacks took place? (5) Did you hear or see anything suspicious? Anyone who (6) has any information and can help the police should phone Brentford 701. This man is dangerous. (7) He has attacked before.

ANNE: (1) **Suppose you recognised that man,** what would you do?

DEREK: What do you mean?

ANNE: Well, (2) ______________________________ or, even worse, (3) ______________________________, would you tell the police?

DEREK: But I don't know him, so the question isn't relevant, is it?

ANNE: Well, all right. But just (4) ______________________________ when the attacks took place. (5) ______________________________, would you phone that number?

DEREK: I don't know and I'm not really interested.

ANNE: OK. But (6) ______________________________ and ______________________________ to catch the man, surely it would be your duty to tell them?

DEREK: Well, possibly.

ANNE: What do you mean 'possibly'! Just (7) ______________________________ you instead of those old ladies, what then?

DEREK: Attacked me? Well, that would be different, wouldn't it?

EXERCISE 5

Complete the sentences by choosing from boxes A, B *and* C *below and putting the verb into the correct form. The first one has been done for you.*

A	B	C
as if as though	live be have commit win say run	a fortune a crime something terrible the company a palace a complete idiot all the time in the world

1 You know we're in a terrible hurry, but you act **as if we had all the time in the world**!

2 He's only an office clerk, but he behaves ______________ he ______________________!

3 OK, I made a mistake, but there's no need to treat me ______________ I ______________________!

4 She only won £100, but she talks ____________ she ______________________!

5 I only said I didn't like it. There's no need to look at me ____________ I ______________________!

6 It's only a small two-bedroomed house, but she talks ____________ she ______________________!

7 Look, I'm sorry I forgot your birthday, but do stop behaving ____________ I ______________________!

11 TO + INFINITIVE/INFINITIVE WITHOUT TO

BIRD'S EYE BOX: To + infinitive/infinitive without to

Would you like **something to eat**?	→	object + **to** + infinitive (Exercises 1 and 8)
It's too **hot to drink**.	→	adjective + **to** + infinitive (Exercises 2, 3 and 8)
I don't know **how to thank** you.	→	question word + **to** + infinitive (Exercise 4)
I've come **to see** the manager.	→	**to** + infinitive (purpose) (Exercise 5)
I've **decided to change** my job.	→	verbs followed by **to** + infinitive (Exercise 8)
Let me **speak**! **Make** him **be** quiet!	→	**let/make** + infinitive (Exercises 6 and 8)
I heard him **come** in.	→	verbs of perception + infinitive (Exercises 7 and 8)
You **mustn't make** a noise.	→	modals + infinitive (Exercise 8)

EXERCISE 1

Choose a suitable verb to complete the following. Sometimes more than one verb would be appropriate. The first one has been done for you.

1 Sandra! I've got something **to tell** you!

2 Sorry, I'll have to go now. I've got a train ______________.

3 Excuse me, sir. There's a Mr Thatcher ______________ you.

4 I'm afraid I can't come out tonight. I've got too much homework ______________.

5 I'll have to buy a new dress. We're going to a party on Saturday and I've got nothing ______________.

6 At the moment I'm staying with friends, but I'm looking for a flat __________.

7 It was so embarrassing! They asked me to make a speech, but I couldn't think of anything __________!

8 Do I have to make a decision now, or can I have a few days __________ about it?

EXERCISE 2

The following letter was published in a newspaper. Complete the letter by choosing the appropriate verb from the box below. Do not use any verb more than once. The first one has been done for you.

be	employ	give	have	learn	let	read	say	work

Dear Sir,

I was not at all surprised (1) **to read** in the paper that there are now more unemployed young people than ever before. If I were a boss, I'd be very reluctant (2) __________ anyone under twenty-five. What can school-leavers offer an employer? They're too young (3) __________ any experience, and, I'm sorry (4) __________, most of them are too lazy (5) __________ hard! They are quite happy (6) __________ the State look after them, because the State is foolish enough (7) __________ them money for doing nothing!

Yours faithfully,

A. J. Williams

EXERCISE 3

Join each of the following pairs of sentences to make one sentence and then complete the letter below. The first one has been done for you.

1 I read the letter from A. J. Williams. I was extremely angry.

2 He says that young people are lazy. This is stupid.

3 They don't have any experience. They aren't old enough.

4 Employers don't offer them jobs. Employers are unwilling.

5 Young people learn. They are quick.

6 They work hard. They are keen.

7 You see young people out of work. This is very sad.

8 The young won't look for jobs. They'll be too depressed.

> Dear Sir,
>
> (1) I was **extremely angry to read the letter from A. J. Williams**. (2) It is ______________________.
> Of course (3) they ______________________, but how can they get experience if (4) employers ______________________?
> (5) Young people ______________________ and (6) they ______________________. I think (7) it is ______________________.
> If the situation doesn't change soon, (8) the young ______________________.
>
> Yours faithfully,
>
> E. F. Bonner

EXERCISE 4

David was driving his car one evening when he had a puncture. He is telling his friend about it. Complete the following by choosing the correct question word from the box on the left and the appropriate verb from the box on the right. Do not use any verb more than once. The first one has been done for you.

where which what who how whether	ask change do go join leave say stay tell

Well, I knew I had to do something, but I didn't know (1) **what to do**. I suppose most people can change a wheel themselves, but I had no idea (2) ________________ it. You see, I'm not very mechanical. So I thought I'd better ask someone to help me, but I couldn't decide (3) ________________. I mean, you feel so stupid! Anyway, I decided I'd have to go to a garage, but, not knowing the area very well, I wasn't sure (4) ________________. It's my own fault, I know. I should have joined one of those motoring organisations, like the A A or the R A C. The trouble is, I could never decide (5) ________________. I mean, they both have their advantages and disadvantages, don't they? Anyway, there I was on a Saturday evening, wondering (6) ________________ in the car or look for a garage, when a young woman stopped and asked if she could help. Imagine my surprise when, in a few minutes, she'd changed the wheel for me! Well, I was speechless! I just didn't know (7) ________________!

EXERCISE 5

Yesterday Linda made a list of the various things she had to do. Read the list and then complete the sentences below. Sometimes more than one answer is acceptable.

1 Times of trains to Oxford?
2 Library – books back.
3 Marino's – table for two on Saturday.
4 Post Office – stamps.
5 Hairdresser's – appointment Friday p.m.
6 Bank – £50.
7 Dental appointment, 10.30 Tuesday – cancel.
8 Anne – come to lunch on Sunday?

Example: Doctor's – prescription.
She went to the doctor's **to collect a prescription**.

1 She phoned the station ________________ the times of the trains to Oxford.

2 She went to the ________________.

3 She phoned ________________.

4 She went ____.

5 She rang ____.

6 She went ____.

7 She phoned ____.

8 She rang ____.

EXERCISE 6

Read the following conversation. Decide first if you should use **let** *or* **make** *and then choose the appropriate verb from the box below to complete the conversation. Do not use any verb more than once. The first one has been done for you.*

ache	do	drink	eat	feel	have	know	laugh	make	think

PENNY: I hear you spent a week at a health farm. What was it like?

HELEN: Absolutely dreadful! They (1) **make you do** exercises from morning till night and they don't (2) ______________ you ______________ anything except for grapefruit. It was worse than being in prison!

PENNY: But did it do you any good?

HELEN: Oh yes! I lost twelve kilos and I feel much better! In fact, I'm going back next month.

PENNY: Oh, Helen, you do (3) ______________ me ______________! You're so funny! I'm sure it wasn't as bad as all that!

HELEN: No, I suppose not. To be honest, it was quite enjoyable, especially the sauna. That (4) ______________ you ______________ marvellous! But, if you're not used to doing anything energetic, the exercises really (5) ______________ your legs ______________ by the end of the day.

PENNY: I've often wondered what health farms are like.

HELEN: Well, I've got a booklet about it at home. I'll (6) ______________ you ______________ a look at it, if you like. If you're interested, why don't you come with me next month?

PENNY: Well, I might, but (7) ______________ me ______________ about it first. It sounds like hard work! Oh! All right! I'll have a look at the booklet and then I'll (8) ______________ you ______________ later!

EXERCISE 7

A sports reporter interviewed several people about an incident involving two players, Foreman and Sherriff, in a football match. He wrote down statements made by each of them. Join each of the following pairs of sentences to make one sentence and then complete the newspaper report that follows. The first one has been done for you.

TURNER:	**1**	Foreman deliberately knocked Sherriff down. I saw him.
FOREMAN:	**2**	Sherriff fell down. I noticed him.
	3	The referee blew his whistle. I didn't hear him.
CARSTON:	**4**	Sherriff tripped over. I saw that.
	5	But did Foreman touch him? I didn't notice.
SHERRIFF:	**6**	Someone shouted. I heard him.
	7	Someone pushed me from behind. I felt it.
FOOTBALL SUPPORTER:	**8**	Foreman's played lots of matches. I've watched him.
	9	He's never fouled before. At least, I've never seen him.

Football Star Sent Off

There was a storm of protest yesterday after referee Sam Turner sent off top player Tim Foreman for fouling against Bob Sherriff. After the match Turner said, (1) '**I saw Foreman deliberately knock Sherriff down.** I blew my whistle, but Foreman ignored it, so I showed him the red card.' Foreman angrily denied this, saying, (2) 'I ____________________, but I never touched him. I carried on playing because (3) ____________________.' Team-mate Willie Carston agreed with Foreman when he said, 'I shouted at Foreman to pass me the ball. Then (4) ____________________, but (5) ____________________.' Sherriff refused to speak to reporters, but his manager said, (6) 'Sherriff ____________________ and then (7) he ____________________. There was definitely a foul.' Foreman supporters found it hard to believe. As one supporter put it, (8) '____________________, but (9) ____________________.'

EXERCISE 8

Ron Blakelock has been dismissed from his job for hitting one of the managers, Mr Cowley. The other workers are on strike because they believe Mr Cowley started the trouble. Complete the following discussion by using the verb in brackets as an infinitive with or without **to**. *The first one has been done for you.*

TOM: Now, I've spoken to the Managing Director, and he seems (1) **to be** (be) ready (2) ______________ (listen) to our side of the story. In fact, he's offered (3) ______________ (talk) to us, but only if we agree (4) ______________ (go) back to work immediately. I said I'd let him (5) ______________ (know) our decision after this meeting. Well, have you got anything (6) ______________ (say)?

BERT: Yes, I have. I'm not returning to work until he promises (7) ______________ (give) Ron his job back. And no one can (8) ______________ (make) me! After all, that's why we're on strike, isn't it?

TOM: No one's going to make you (9) ______________ (do) anything, Bert. But you must (10) ______________ (remember) that it's a difficult situation. Everyone saw Ron (11) ______________ (hit) Mr Cowley. There's no doubt about that. The question is why he hit him. We hope (12) ______________ (show) that it was Mr Cowley's own fault. But we can't (13) ______________ (do) that if the management refuses (14) ______________ (discuss) it with us, can we?

DAVE: Tom's right, Bert. Frankly, I think we should (15) ______________ (do) what the Managing Director says. It's not very sensible (16) ______________ (stay) on strike under the circumstances. It won't help Ron (17) ______________ (get) his job back, will it?

BERT: I still don't like it. We all know what Mr Cowley said to Ron.

TOM: Yes, but no one heard him (18) ______________ (say) it, did they? It's Ron's word against Mr Cowley's. Look, let's (19) ______________ (have) a vote. Anyone who wishes (20) ______________ (continue) the strike, put up your hand. Well, it looks as if the majority wants (21) ______________ (return) to work. What about you, Bert? What have you decided (22) ______________ (do)?

BERT: You needn't (23) ______________ (worry). I intend (24) ______________ (accept) the majority decision.

TOM: Good. Now, I've got a lot of things (25) ______________ (do) first, but I'll arrange for us (26) ______________ (meet) the Managing Director as soon as possible. In the meantime, I'll tell him he can (27) ______________ (expect) (28) ______________ (see) us back at work tomorrow.

12 GERUND

BIRD'S EYE BOX: Gerund

Cycling is good exercise.	→	as a subject (Exercises 1, 2 and 6)
What do you fancy **doing**? You promised **to help** me.	→	gerund or **to** + infinitive (Exercises 3 and 6)
He left without **saying** goodbye.	→	after prepositions (Exercises 4 and 6)
He's **trying to start** the car. (Aim) Has he **tried checking** the oil? (Method)	→	verbs followed by **to** + infinitive or gerund, with different meanings (Exercises 5 and 6)

EXERCISE 1

Join the two sentences to make one sentence, beginning with a gerund.

Example: She's a nurse. It's hard work.
Being a nurse is hard work.
or **Nursing is hard work.**

1 She looks after young children. It's very tiring.

2 He didn't get the job. It depressed him.

3 They share a flat. This sometimes causes arguments.

4 She's a teacher. It requires a lot of patience.

5 He never goes out. That must be boring.

6 He doesn't have any friends. This must make him lonely.

EXERCISE 2

Read the politician's speech and write down his solutions to the problems. The first one has been done for you.

> 'Today we are faced with many problems, both social and economic. What are we, the Government, going to do about them? (1) First of all, we are going to create new jobs. This will reduce unemployment. (2) Then we must export more goods, which will help the economy. Of course, the future of the country is in the hands of the young, (3) so we intend to train more teachers, and this will raise the level of education. (4) We must also provide more entertainment for young people. This will keep them out of trouble. (5) In addition, we plan to cut taxation, and this will help the lower-paid workers. (6) And, finally, we are going to employ more policemen, which will make our streets safer.'

1 **Creating more jobs will reduce unemployment.**

2 ______________________________.

3 ______________________________.

4 ______________________________.

5 ______________________________.

6 ______________________________.

EXERCISE 3

Complete the dialogue with the correct form of the verb in brackets (gerund or **to** *+ infinitive). The first one has been done for you.*

MANAGER: I thought you ought to know, sir, I've decided (1) **to give** (give) in my notice. I hope (2) ______________ (leave) at the end of the month.

DIRECTOR: Thank you for (3) ______________ (let) me know, Dennis, but I can't help (4) ______________ (wonder) why you want (5) ______________ (leave). You've been with this company for ten years now, so you can't dislike (6) ______________ (work) here, surely?

MANAGER: Oh, certainly not, sir. I've really enjoyed (7) ______________ (be) here. It's just . . . well, it's difficult.

DIRECTOR: Yes? Go on.

MANAGER: Well, I didn't want (8) ______________ (say) this, sir, but I just can't stand (9) ______________ (work) with Mr Mitchell, the deputy manager. If I don't leave soon, I'll end up (10) ______________ (do) something I might regret.

DIRECTOR: I see. Would you mind (11) ______________ (tell) me exactly what the problem is?

MANAGER: Well, I don't mean (12) ______________ (be) unfair to him. He's young and ambitious, but he's full of these new ideas. He keeps (13) ______________ (try) to change things.

DIRECTOR: Is that such a bad idea, Dennis?

MANAGER: It is when the men refuse (14) ______________ (work) with him, sir. It's making my life impossible. So, I don't feel like (15) ______________ (stay) with the company under the circumstances.

DIRECTOR: I understand you (16) ______________ (feel) this way, Dennis, and I appreciate you (17) ______________ (tell) me about it. However, I have offered (18) ______________ (transfer) Mr Mitchell to another branch, and I'm expecting his answer this afternoon. I can't promise anything, but if he agrees (19) ______________ (go), perhaps you'd consider (20) ______________ (stay) with the company?

MANAGER: Yes, of course I would, sir.

EXERCISE 4

Read through the news items and fill in the spaces with a suitable word or phrase. The first one has been done for you.

And here is a round-up of the news in brief.

Two men escaped from Durham jail early this morning by (1) **climbing** a wall. Both men were serving five years for (2) ______________________ an elderly man.

Police are looking for a hit-and-run driver who drove off without (3) ______________________ after (4) ______________________ a young woman. Police are interested in (5) ______________________ anyone who saw the accident.

Boxing champion Steve Goddard appeared in court today, accused of (6) ______________________. He was found not guilty. Goddard spoke to reporters before (7) ______________________ and said that he was now looking forward to (8) ______________________.

Pop star Scott Turner plans to retire after his next European tour. He said today he was tired of (9) ______________________ and wanted to spend more time with his family instead of (10) ______________________.

British racing driver Bob Nicolas flew home last night after (11) ______________________ the Brazilian Grand Prix. His car developed engine trouble during the race, and he had difficulty in (12) ______________________.

An Essex grandmother, Mrs Maude Williams, celebrated her 100th birthday today by (13) ______________________ Concorde. She was nervous of (14) ______________________ before the flight, but, on (15) ______________________ Heathrow Airport, she said she'd had a wonderful time and thanked everyone for (16) ______________________.

And, finally, a young man who took his pet snake to a party ended up (17) ______________________ the night at the local police station. Paul Rimmer, twenty-six, said, 'I was worried about (18) ______________________ the snake at home because of the cold. So I put it into a box and left it in a bedroom. It was all right until someone insisted on (19) ______________________ the box and the snake escaped. That's when the police were called.' Mr Rimmer apologised for (20) ______________________ and was later allowed to go home.

EXERCISE 5

Choose the correct words (a or b) to complete the sentence and write the letter in the box provided.

Example: Graham wants to drive to Spain, but I'd prefer ______________.
(a) to fly (b) flying [a]

1 I hope she remembers ______________ him the message when she sees him tonight. It's important.
(a) to give (b) giving [ ]

2 It was such a funny story, I couldn't stop ______________!
(a) to laugh (b) laughing [ ]

3 If you're not getting a good picture on your television, try ______________ the aerial.
(a) to adjust (b) adjusting [ ]

4 She began her career as a model and then she went on ______________ films.
(a) to make (b) making [ ]

5 Now, you remember ______________, but do you remember anything else about the accident?
(a) to skid (b) skidding [ ]

6 I'd hate ______________ into trouble with the police. Wouldn't you?
(a) to get (b) getting [ ]

7 It was a very good flight. We only stopped once _______________ in Kuwait.
(a) to refuel (b) refuelling ☐

8 Although the policeman shouted, 'Stop!', the man went on _______________.
(a) to run (b) running ☐

9 I hate _______________ to get up early. Don't you?
(a) to have (b) having ☐

10 Please make a little less noise. I'm trying _______________.
(a) to concentrate (b) concentrating ☐

EXERCISE 6

Complete the letter with the correct form of the verb in brackets (gerund or **to** *+ infinitive). The first one has been done for you.*

Dear Carol,

Many apologies for not (1) **replying** (reply) to your letter earlier, but I've been awfully busy. Thanks very much for (2) _______________ (invite) me to stay with you over the bank holiday weekend. Of course, I'd love (3) _______________ (come).

However, instead of (4) _______________ (drive) as I usually do, I've decided (5) _______________ (come) by train, as I don't fancy (6) _______________ (sit) in a traffic jam for hours! As you know, (7) _______________ (drive) on a bank holiday is always murder!

I'm planning (8) _______________ (catch) the 8.45 from Waterloo Station, which gets in about eleven o'clock. Please don't worry about (9) _______________ (meet) me at the station. It isn't far to your house, so I don't mind (10) _______________ (walk). In fact, after (11) _______________ (sit) for a couple of hours on a crowded train, I'll enjoy the fresh air!

By the way, I'd like (12) _______________ (bring) something for the children. I was thinking of (13) _______________ (get) them each a book. Do they still like (14) _______________ (read), or would they prefer (15) ______________ (have) something else? What do you think?

I must say, I'm really looking forward to (16) ______________ (see) you again and to (17) ______________ (hear) all your news. I've got some interesting news I want (18) ______________ (tell) you, but it'll have (19) ______________ (wait) until I see you. Anyway, do remember (20) ______________ (let) me know about the children.

See you soon.

Love,

Christine

13 PARTICIPLES

BIRD'S EYE BOX: Participles

It was a **worrying** situation. We were all very **worried**.	→	present and past participles used as adjectives (Exercises 1, 2 and 9)
Students **starting** on Monday should arrive by 8.30. Fees **paid** in advance are not refundable.	→	present and past participles to introduce an adjectival phrase (Exercises 3 and 9)
Sitting in the front row, we had an excellent view.	→	present participle to introduce an adverbial phrase (Exercises 4 and 9)
Opening the door, the cat came in.	→	misrelated participles (Exercise 5)
I noticed him **coming** along the road.	→	present participle after verbs of perception (Exercises 6 and 7)
Having visited the museum, we decided to have lunch in the park.	→	present perfect participle to introduce an adverbial phrase (Exercises 8 and 9)

EXERCISE 1

Complete the following newspaper headlines with the correct form of the verb in brackets.

Examples: Police recover **stolen** (steal) jewellery in Scotland.

Frazer wins championship after **exciting** (excite) match.

1 ______________ (fall) trees block Birmingham–Wolverhampton road.

2 Pilot tells of ______________ (amaze) escape.

3 Government policy blamed for ______________ (rise) prices.

4 Football star in hospital with ______________ (break) leg.

5 Police search for ______________ (miss) child.

6 _____________ (burst) water-pipes cause flooding in central London.

7 _____________ (worry) parents demand meeting with Education Minister.

8 Queen returns home after _____________ (exhaust) tour.

EXERCISE 2

Complete the following newspaper article by putting a circle round the correct word in brackets. The first one has been done for you.

FILM REVIEW

When I first saw his work, I thought David Lennox seemed a (1) (promising / promised) young director. So, I was (2) (interesting/interested) to see his latest film, *Vermilion*. I was not (3) (disappointing/disappointed). The story is very (4) (exciting/excited) the special effects are (5) (astonishing/astonished), and I was most (6) (impressing/impressed) by the photography. Unfortunately, the same cannot be said of *Tell Me Another*, Freddie Dash's latest film. Advertised as 'an original comedy', it is neither original nor (7) (amusing/amused). In fact, some of the jokes are so bad as to be almost (8) (embarrassing/embarrassed). I was not (9) (surprising/surprised) that most of the audience appeared totally (10) (boring/bored) by the end, as the story is most (11) (confusing/confused). I am sorry to say that it is a most (12) (disappointing/disappointed) film.

EXERCISE 3

Complete the following notices and announcements by choosing a verb from the box below and putting it into the correct form (present or past participle). Do not use any verb more than once.

arrive buy damage leave meet wait wear

Example: Passengers <u>**wishing**</u> to smoke should sit at the rear of the bus.

1 The train _____________ at platform two is the 10.43 to Reading.

2 Goods _____________ in transit should be returned to the manufacturer.

3 Cars _____________ in a no-parking zone will be removed.

4 Any guest not _____________ a tie will be asked to leave.

5 Clothes _____________ in the sale cannot be changed.

6 Friends and relatives _____________ passengers from New Delhi are advised that flight BA763 has been delayed.

EXERCISE 4

Read the following extract from a story. Then choose a suitable verb and put it in the correct form to complete the passage. The first one has been done for you.

(1) **Moving** carefully and not (2) ______________ a sound, Douglas slowly made his way towards the window. (3) ______________ through a gap between the curtains, he could see the three men. The fat one, Wiseman, stood by the fireplace, (4) ______________ a cigar and (5) ______________ excitedly to Petersson, the Norwegian. Petersson appeared to be listening intently, (6) ______________ from time to time as if Wiseman had said something funny. The third man, Wescott, sat on the sofa, (7) ______________ the paper, not (8) ______________ the other two. Suddenly, the door opened and a fourth man came in, (9) ______________ a large suitcase, which he put down on the table. As Douglas stood (10) ______________ the four men in the room, he heard a sound behind him. (11) ______________ round, he could just see in the darkness the shape of a man only a few metres away. (12) ______________ his gun out of his jacket, Douglas stepped into the shadow of a tree and waited.

EXERCISE 5

Read the following sentences and decide which are acceptable and which are not. Put a tick (√) or a cross (X) in the appropriate box and then correct those you find unacceptable.

Example: Answering the phone, the toast burnt. [X]
While I was answering the phone, the toast burnt.

1 Driving along the road, a car pulled out in front of me. [ ]

2 Reading the book a second time, I understood it better. [ ]

3 Hidden in the wood, the police found a body. [ ]

4 Looking left and right, the traffic slowed down and she crossed the road. [ ]

5 Exhausted by the journey, he went straight to bed. [ ]

6 Walking across the golf course, a golf ball hit him. [ ]

EXERCISE 6

A film director is talking to some actors about the scene they are going to film. Use the notes below to complete his directions. The first one has been done for you.

1 watch/children/play	**5** see/shark/come
2 look at/some girls/sunbathe	**6** hear/Rita/shout
3 see/something/move	**7** feel/surfboard/rock
4 notice/Dave/windsurf	**8** hear/Dave/scream

OK. Now, the next scene is on the beach, and we want to create a nice, peaceful atmosphere. Rita, you're (1) **watching the children playing** in the water, and Peter, you're (2) ______________________ farther along the beach, through your binoculars. OK? Suddenly, Rita, you (3) ______________________ through the water. You borrow Peter's binoculars to see more clearly, and then you realise it's a shark. At the same time, you (4) ______________________ near by. That's when you start shouting. Right? Now, Dave, you don't (5) ______________________ towards you and you're too far away to (6) ______________________. The first time you realise something is wrong is when you (7) ______________________. You lose your balance and fall in. The scene finishes with the reaction of the people on the beach when they (8) ______________________. Clear? Right, quiet, everybody.

EXERCISE 7

You spent the night in a house where strange things happened. Use the ideas below to make sentences about what you ***saw, heard*** *and* ***felt****.*

Examples: Someone screamed.
I heard someone scream.

A figure was dancing in the garden.
I saw a figure dancing in the garden.

1 Someone was crying in the next room.
2 A cold hand touched me.
3 Something was floating in the air above my head.
4 A door slammed suddenly.
5 A white face appeared and then disappeared.
6 Something was crawling up my arm.
7 The wind was howling outside.
8 Someone tapped me on the shoulder.

EXERCISE 8

Read the following speech by the prosecution at a murder trial. Then choose a suitable verb and put it in the correct form to complete the speech. The first one has been done for you.

Ladies and gentlemen of the jury, I intend to prove to you that the defendant, Michael Perkins, cold-bloodedly decided to kill Penelope Hennessy for money, and that, (1) **having made** that decision, he set about planning exactly how to kill her. I will show that, (2) ______________________ the murder in detail, he carried it out on the night of October 26th, when he shot Mrs Hennessy through the heart. I will produce evidence to show that, (3) ______________________ Mrs Hennessy, he disposed of the body in the New Forest and that, (4) ______________________ the body, he drove to Lymington, where he threw the gun in the sea. (5) ______________________ the gun, he drove back to the house to remove any evidence of the crime. (6) ______________________ sure that there was nothing to connect him with Mrs Hennessy's disappearance, he took several thousand pounds from the safe and hid it in the churchyard at Lyndhurst. (7) ______________________ the money, he returned to his own house. So far, he had committed the perfect crime. But, (8) ______________________ the perfect crime, he became careless and began to make mistakes. I now call the first witness for the prosecution.

EXERCISE 9

Complete the sentences with the correct form of the verb in brackets. The first one has been done for you.

1 I found it difficult to follow the serial, **having missed** (miss) the first episode.

2 ______________________ (annoy) by the constant interruptions, the Minister refused to continue, ______________________ (demand) that the trouble-makers leave.

3 Anyone ______________________ (travel) without a ticket may be fined up to £100.

4 She cut her foot on a piece of ______________________ (break) glass, half ______________________ (hide) in the sand.

5 ______________________ (realise) he'd missed the bus, Patrick began to walk home, ______________________ (hope) another bus would come before long.

6 ______________________ (take) the machine to pieces, Alan found he couldn't put it together again.

7 The river, ______________________ (swell) by the heavy rain, burst its banks and flooded the ______________________ (surround) countryside.

8 ______________________ (lie) in bed, ______________________ (worry) and ______________________ (depress), Sarah started to think once again about the problem.

9 Students ______________________ (want) to take the exam should give their names to the Principal by Friday.

10 She didn't want to hear the story again, ______________________ (hear) it all before.

14 THE PASSIVE

BIRD'S EYE BOX: The Passive

He **was asked** to leave. She**'s been given** promotion.	→	different tenses of the passive (Exercises 1, 2, 3 and 8)
He was attacked **by a madman.** He was attacked **with an axe.**	→	**by** or **with** + agent (Exercise 3)
It **shouldn't be allowed**! It **must be used** with care.	→	modal passives (Exercises 4, 5 and 8)
The money **is to be given** to charity.	→	passive infinitive (Exercises 6 and 7)

EXERCISE 1

Complete the following by choosing from boxes A + C *or* A + B + C. *Use each verb once only. The first one has been done for you.*

A	B	C
is/are was/were has/have had	going to be being been	changed delayed held up kept offered pulled down repaired used warned

1 All flights from Gatwick **have been delayed** because of the weather.

2 Sorry we're late. We ____________________ in the traffic.

3 Why can't you go down Station Road? ______ the road ________________?

4 I really can't sympathise with Graham. He knew what would happen if he did it again, as he ____________________ before.

5 Is the dialling code for Orpington still 66, or ____________ the number ____________?

6 I intended to go to the car-wash on the way home, but when I got there it ________________________, and I didn't have time to wait.

7 You won't find the encyclopaedias in here. They ________________________ in the reference library.

8 You can't blame Michael for leaving. I understand he ________________________ a far better job.

9 I hear the old primary school ________________________ soon. Apparently, they want to build a block of flats on the land.

EXERCISE 2

Complete the following news items by putting the verb in brackets into the correct form. The first one has been done for you.

1 Two men (a) **are being questioned** (question) at Marylebone Police Station tonight in connection with last week's armed robbery in Luton, in which £25,000 (b) ________________________ (steal) from a Securicor van. Another man (c) ________________________ already ________________________ (arrest) for the crime.

2 Four people (a) ________________________ (take) to hospital after a fire at their home in Tottenham early this morning. They (b) ________________________ (send) home after treatment for minor burns. Police believe the fire (c) ________________________ (start) deliberately.

3 Disc jockey Paul Asherton (a) ________________________ (ban) from driving for two years. The court (b) ________________________ (tell) that it was the third time Asherton (c) ________________________ (stop) for speeding in six months. Asherton admitted driving at more than 125 m.p.h.

4 Missing schoolgirl Sheila Patterson, aged eleven, (a) ________________________ (find) alive and well in Leicester. Sheila, who disappeared two days ago, said she had left home to join a circus. Her parents are travelling to Leicester tonight. Meanwhile, Sheila (b) ________________________ (look) after at Leicester Police Station.

5 Lorry-driver Albert Whittaker had a lucky escape this afternoon when a concrete block, which (a) ______________ (load) on to his lorry, fell off and landed inches from his feet. Mr Whittaker (b) ______________ (treat) for shock.

EXERCISE 3

Complete the second sentence so that it means the same as the first, using **by** *or* **with** *only where necessary.*

Example: The police believe that someone used a master key to open the door.
The police believe that the **door was opened with a master key**.

1 Adrian Holt, the well-known composer, is writing the music.
The music ______________.

2 Apparently, someone used a knife to kill her.
Apparently, she ______________.

3 The police have arrested a 39-year-old mother of three for shop-lifting.
A 39-year-old ______________.

4 Ice on the road almost certainly caused the accident.
The ______________.

5 I haven't got my car at the moment. The garage is repairing it.
I haven't got my car at the moment. It ______________.

6 The supermarket manager was afraid that someone had injected poison into some of the food.
The supermarket manager was afraid that some of ______________.

EXERCISE 4

Use the following sentences to write notices in the boxes below. The first one has been done for you.

1 'You must keep dogs on a lead.'

Dogs must be kept on a lead.

2 'You should collect prescriptions before midday.'

3 'We will arrest shop-lifters.'

4 'You can borrow tennis-rackets on request.'

5 'You may not take reference books out of the library.'

6 'You must not remove these instructions.'

EXERCISE 5

Use the following to complete the extract from a radio programme below. The first one has been done for you.

1 We have to do something.
2 What can we do?
3 We could solve the problem.
4 We have to improve the public transport system.
5 We ought to reduce fares.
6 The Government should provide more money.
7 It would encourage people to leave their cars at home.
8 We need to introduce higher car-park charges.
9 We ought to employ more traffic wardens.
10 It would discourage drivers.
11 Will they do anything about the problem?
12 We must find a solution quickly.

London in the rush-hour! Everyone complains about it, don't they? And everyone agrees that (1) **something has to be done**. But (2) ______________________ about the endless traffic jams, the late trains and the overcrowded buses? We've been out to ask people in the street how they think (3) ______________________. Nearly everyone feels that (4) ______________________ and that (5) ______________________. To do this, they say that (6) ______________________, and then (7) ______________________. Other people feel that (8) ______________________ and (9) ______________________ so that (10) ______________________ from taking their cars into the city centre. But (11) ______________________________ in the near future? We hope so, because (12) ______________________________. Otherwise, one day soon, London's traffic will come to a complete standstill.

EXERCISE 6

Use the following sentences to write instructions in the boxes below. The first one has been done for you.

1 'Dilute this in water.'

To be diluted in water.

2 'Take these after meals.'

3 'Do not give to children under five.'

4 'Use only with soft contact lenses.'

5 'Do not spray near eyes or mouth.'

6 'Do not use on broken or sensitive skin.'

EXERCISE 7

Complete the following newspaper reports by choosing a suitable verb from the box below and putting it into the correct form. Do not use any verb more than once. The first one has been done for you.

build	give	increase	lead	open	return	take over

1

The Government is to set up an inquiry into the Mortlake train crash. The inquiry **is to be led** by the Minister of Transport, Frank Vine.

2

Two firemen, who saved the life of a sixteen-year-old girl, ______________________ a medal for bravery.

3

Buffers, the fast-food chain, ______________________ by the American supermarket Sellwell.

4

British Rail announced today that fares ______________ ________ by five per cent from April.

5

In an agreement between the British and Italian governments, the Venetian Statues, at present in the British Museum, ______________________ to Italy.

6

Steadfast Manor, the home of Lord and Lady Steadfast, ______________________ to the public in June.

EXERCISE 8

Read the following extract from an adventure story. Then complete the extract by putting the verbs in brackets into the correct form. There may sometimes be more than one possible answer. The first one has been done for you.

Jake felt sure that the secret plans (1) **were hidden** (hide) somewhere in the room. He began searching carefully. Behind a picture on the wall he found a small metal safe. 'They (2) ______________________ (keep) in here,' he thought. Suddenly, he (3) ______________________ (push) violently from behind. He fell, hitting his head on the stone floor, and everything went black.

When he came round, he found that he (4) ______________________ (take) to a small room. His hands and feet (5) ______________________ (tie) with rope and he felt as if he (6) ______________________ (drug). He also had the strange feeling that he (7) ______________________ (watch). A few minutes later the door (8) ______________________ (unlock), and two men walked into the room. Jake immediately recognised one of them. It was Boris Mariovitch, the mad scientist!

'So, my friend,' said Boris, smiling coldly, 'what made you think the plans (9) ______________________ (keep) in the safe? You fool! They (10) ______________________ (hide) where no one will ever find them!'

'What are you going to do with him?' asked the second man, pointing at Jake.

'Him? Nothing for the moment. No doubt he (11) ______________________ (kill) in the morning!'

The two men left. The door slammed shut and (12) ______________________ (lock) from the outside. Jake looked desperately round the room. The door (13) ______________________ (make) of metal and (14) ______________________ (not break). The windows (15) ______________________ (not open) from the inside. What was he going to do? There was no escape! Jake (16) ______________________ (trap)!

15 QUESTION TAGS

BIRD'S EYE BOX: Question tags

He isn't very old, **is he**?	→	positive tags (Exercises 1, 2, 3 and 4)
You've been to Spain, **haven't you**?	→	negative tags (Exercises 1, 2, 3 and 4)
They must be very rich, **mustn't they**?	→	modal tags (Exercises 1, 2, 3 and 4)
You locked the door, **didn't you**?	→	intonation in question tags (Exercise 4)
You locked the door, **didn't you**?		

EXERCISE 1

Complete the following with the correct question tags.

Examples: You won't be long, **will you?**

Nobody saw you, **did they?**

1 He's got a very good job, ______?

2 Well, you'd better tell me about it, ______?

3 I couldn't borrow your dictionary, ______?

4 I am right, ______?

5 That wasn't a very diplomatic thing to say, ______?

6 You'll be home early tonight, ______?

7 Everyone's gone home now, ______?

8 No one really likes him, ______?

9 You'd like to see it, ______?

EXERCISE 2

Mr Hardwick, a driving instructor, is giving a driving lesson to seventeen-year-old Gary. Complete the following dialogue with the correct question tags. The first one has been done for you.

INSTRUCTOR: Now, you remember what you learned last lesson, (1) **don't you?**

GARY: Yes, of course. Start the engine, into first gear, and we're off. That was all right, (2) ________________?

INSTRUCTOR: Not really. You didn't indicate, (3) ________________?

GARY: Oh, sorry, I forgot. Still, it doesn't really matter, (4) ________________?

INSTRUCTOR: That's where you're wrong, Gary. I'm afraid it does matter.

GARY: Well, I can't be expected to remember everything, (5) ________________? It's only my third lesson, after all.

INSTRUCTOR: OK, Gary. Anyway, watch your speed. You're going too fast.

GARY: But I'm only doing thirty-five m.p.h!

INSTRUCTOR: I know, but this is a built-up area, (6) ____________? And there's a thirty m.p.h. speed limit.

GARY: But look at everyone else. They're all going faster than thirty m.p.h., (7) ________________?

INSTRUCTOR: That doesn't make any difference. You haven't passed your test yet, (8) ________________? Now, turn right at the next corner and – Gary, be careful!

GARY: Oh! I shouldn't have done that, (9) ________________?

INSTRUCTOR: No, you certainly shouldn't have! You just weren't concentrating, (10) ________________? Now, for goodness sake, pay attention!

GARY: You don't really like teaching me to drive, (11) ________________, Mr Hardwick?

INSTRUCTOR: It's not a question of liking or disliking, Gary. It's my job. But if you want to pass the test, you'll just have to learn to concentrate, (12) ________________? Now, let's try again.

EXERCISE 3

How many logical and grammatically correct sentences can you make from the following table?

Example: **You have got the keys, haven't you?**

You Patrick They Everyone We It	have will must is were might are would	(not)	have missed the train here got the keys be very nice paid the bill tell her thinking come late	have will must is were might are would	(not)	he? we? you? it? they?

EXERCISE 4

Complete the following with correct question tags. Look at the intonation marks and write in the box which meaning (a, b or c) is probably being expressed.

a You expect agreement.
b You are not sure.
c You are showing surprise.

1 It's Tuesday, **isn't it**? ↗↘ [a]

2 It was terribly crowded, ________________? ↗↘ [ ]

3 You didn't really say that, ________________? ↘↗ [ ]

4 You do like it, ________________? ↘↗ [ ]

5 It is Tuesday, ________________? ↘↗ [ ]

6 He doesn't really want the job, ________________? ↗↘ [ ]

7 I did give you the keys, ________________? ↘↗ [ ]

8 You haven't finished already, ________________? ↘↗ [ ]

9 You can see what I mean, ________________? ↗↘ [ ]

10 You wouldn't honestly do that, ________________? ↘↗ [ ]

16 CONDITIONALS

BIRD'S EYE BOX: Conditionals

I'll send you a card **if** you **give** me your address.	→	first conditional (Exercises 1, 2, 7, 10 and 11)
		CONDITIONAL LINKING WORDS
Supposing he doesn't like it?	→	**supposing, provided that, unless, in case, as long as, so long as** (Exercises 3, 4, 7 and 11)
If I **knew** where he was, **I'd (would) tell** you.	→	second conditional (Exercises 5, 6, 7, 10 and 11)
If he**'d (had) been** more careful, he **wouldn't have broken** it.	→	third conditional (Exercises 8, 9, 10 and 11)

EXERCISE 1

Complete the following pieces of conversation, overheard in a shop, by putting the verbs in brackets into the correct form.

Example: 'If you <u>leave</u> (leave) it with me now, it <u>won't take</u> (not take) more than a couple of days to repair.'

1 'If you ______________ (wait) a minute, sir, I ______________ (see) if the manager ______________ (be) free.'

2 'If it ______________ (not fit), madam, ______________ (bring) it back and we ______________ (change) it.'

3 '______________ I ______________ (get) any discount if I ______________ (pay) cash?'

4 'If you ______________ (give) me your phone number, sir, we ______________ (let) you know when it ______________ (arrive).'

5 'How long ______________ it ______________ (take) if you ______________ (order) one for me?'

6 'If you ______________ (not see) what you ______________ (want), sir, just ______________ (ask) one of the assistants.'

EXERCISE 2

Some workers are demonstrating outside their factory. Use their demands to decide what they actually say to the managers and then complete the exercise below. The first one has been done for you.

1

PAY US MORE MONEY
OR
WE GO ON STRIKE!

2

GIVE US LONGER
HOLIDAYS OR WE DON'T
COME TO WORK!

3

DON'T SHORTEN OUR
LUNCH-BREAK OR WE
WALK OUT!

4

IMPROVE SAFETY
STANDARDS OR WE STOP
WORK!

5

PROVIDE BETTER
WORKING CONDITIONS OR
WE DON'T DO OVERTIME!

6

INTRODUCE A SHORTER
WORKING WEEK OR WE
COMPLAIN TO THE UNION!

1 **If you don't pay us more money, we'll go on strike!**

2 ____!

3 ____!

4 ____!

5 ____!

6 ____!

EXERCISE 3

The managers of the factory are considering the workers' demands. Complete the following sentences by choosing words from the box below. Use each one once only. (Occasionally there is more than one possibility.) The first one has been done for you.

provided (that) supposing as long as so long as unless in case

1 We'll pay them more money **so long as** they work harder.

2 We won't give them longer holidays ______________ they promise to be more productive.

3 We won't shorten their lunch-break ______________ they agree to start earlier.

4 We'll have to improve safety standards ______________ someone has an accident.

5 We'll consider providing better working conditions ______________ we have enough money.

6 ______________ we introduce a shorter working week, how will we make a profit?

EXERCISE 4

Think of a suitable way to complete the second half of the dialogues.

Example: 'Do you think Patrick has much chance of passing the exam?'
'Not unless **he works harder**.'

1 'We don't need to take a map, do we?'
'But supposing ______________________________?'

2 'Can I borrow the car?'
'Yes, so long as ______________________________.'

3 'Do you think I should send it registered post?'
'It might be a good idea, just in case ______________________________.'

4 'So, you're thinking of buying that second-hand car?'
'Well, as long as ______________________________.'

5 'I hear you're planning to go camping next weekend.'
'We hope to, provided that ______________________________.'

6 'Do you think we'll still catch the train?'
'Well, we won't unless ______________________________.'

EXERCISE 5

Arthur Rainer has a lot of bad habits, which he should give up, but it's probably too late for him to change. Use the ideas to complete the exercise below, explaining why he should change his habits. The first one has been done for you.

1 Give up smoking and be healthier!
2 Go on a diet and lose weight!
3 Take some exercise and get fit!
4 Stop drinking and live longer!
5 Eat the right food and feel better!
6 Take care of your health and enjoy life more!

1 **If he gave up smoking, he'd be healthier.**

2 ______________________________.

3 ______________________________.

4 ______________________________.

5 ______________________________.

6 ______________________________.

EXERCISE 6

Complete the following radio programme by putting the verbs in brackets into the correct form. The first one has been done for you.

INTERVIEWER: Welcome once again to our weekly programme in which we ask the questions 'If you (1) **were** (be) alone on a tropical island for a month, what two items (2) ______________ you ______________ (choose) to take with you and why?' My two guests today are racing driver Paul Bartlett and journalist Anna Spall. Paul?

PAUL: Well, I think I (3) ______________ (get) very bored on this island if I (4) ______________ (not have) anything to do. So, I (5) ______________ (take) a knife and a ball of string. Then I (6) ______________ (be able) to make useful things to catch food and, maybe, build some kind of house to live in.

INTERVIEWER: (7) ______________ you ______________ (try) to escape from the island?

PAUL: If I (8) ______________ (manage) to make a boat, I think I (9) ______________ (try).

INTERVIEWER: Anna, what about you?

ANNA: Well, I definitely (10) ______________ (not try) to escape! I'm totally impractical. So, if I (11) ______________ (try) to make anything, I'm sure it (12) ______________________ (fall) to pieces very quickly! No, if I (13) ______________________ (have) to spend a month on this island, I (14) ______________________ (want) to have a good book and a pair of sunglasses!

PAUL: But how (15) ______________________ you ______________________ (catch) things to eat if you (16) ______________________ (not have) any tools?

ANNA: Oh, I expect there (17) ______________________ (be) plenty of fruit on the island. And I'm sure it (18) ______________________ (not hurt) me if I (19) ______________________ (not eat) meat or fish for a month.

INTERVIEWER: (20) ______________________ either of you ______________ (be) lonely?

PAUL: Yes, definitely. I (21) ______________________ (find) it very difficult if I (22) ______________________ (not speak) to anyone for a month.

ANNA: I think I (23) ______________________ (enjoy) the peace and quiet at first, but after a couple of weeks, yes, I (24) ______________________ (begin) to feel lonely.

INTERVIEWER: Paul and Anna, thank you very much.

EXERCISE 7

Complete the clauses in box A by joining each one with a suitable clause from box B to give a logical and grammatically correct sentence. The first one has been done for you.

A	B
1 If he phones while I'm out	so long as you promise not to tell anyone.
2 I wouldn't say it	provided you pay the rent on time!
3 Supposing we rented a car	please take a message.
4 I'll tell you what he said	I'll give you the spare key.
5 In case you're home before me	unless it were true.
6 If you paid more attention	as long as you don't make too much noise.
7 You can have the room for as long as you like	would you be prepared to share the driving?
8 I don't mind you having a party	you'd know what I was talking about!

1 **If he phones while I'm out, please take a message.**

2 ______________________________.

3 ______________________________.

4 ______________________________.

5 ______________________________.

6 ______________________________.

7 ______________________________.

8 ______________________________.

EXERCISE 8

Three drivers are involved in an accident. Read what they say and then complete their statements to the police. The first one has been done for you.

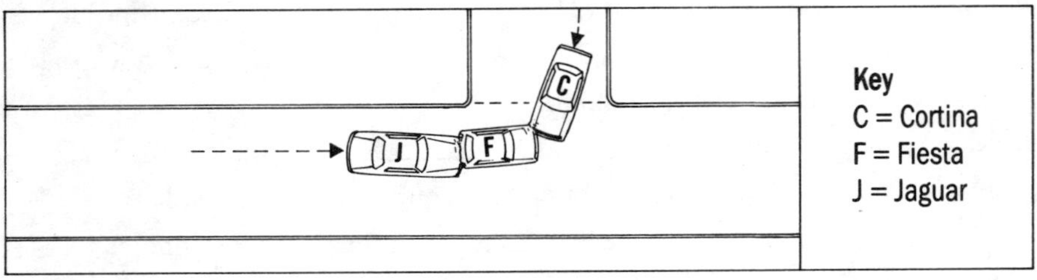

CORTINA DRIVER:
1 He didn't use his headlights. That's why I didn't see him.
2 I didn't see him. That's why I pulled out.

FIESTA DRIVER:
3 He didn't look carefully. That's why he didn't see me.
4 He pulled out in front of me. That's why I had to brake suddenly.
5 The Jaguar was so close behind me. That's why the driver wasn't able to stop.

JAGUAR DRIVER:
6 The driver in front braked suddenly. That's why I hit him.
7 I wanted to overtake him. That's why I was so close behind him.
8 He was such a slow driver. That's why I wanted to overtake him.

These are the statements the drivers made to the police. (Don't forget that some of them are negative.)

CORTINA DRIVER: 1 **If he'd used his headlights, I would have seen him.**

2 ______________________________.

FIESTA DRIVER: 3 ______________________________.

4 ______________________________.

5 ______________________________.

JAGUAR DRIVER: 6 ______________________________.

7 ______________________________.

8 ______________________________.

EXERCISE 9

Read the following news items and then complete what the people say. There is often more than one acceptable answer. The first one has been done for you.

1

An elderly woman was reunited with the son she had not seen for twenty years after recognising his photograph in a national newspaper. 'It was pure chance,' said Mrs Vera Hemmings. '**If I hadn't recognised his photo, we'd never have met again**!'

2

Part of a school roof blew off in high winds yesterday and landed inches from people waiting in a bus queue. Mrs Hilda Vale, fifty-nine, said 'We were terribly lucky.

____

______________________________.'

3

Two yachtsmen were rescued last night after getting into difficulty in heavy seas. Coastguards criticised the two men for not listening to the weather reports. 'These people make me very angry,' said John Smythe, a coastguard,

'______________________________

______________________________.'

4

Middle-weight boxing champion Ally Frazer lost the world title last night when he was knocked out in round six. His manager said, 'He's been working very hard recently. He's tired and his reactions aren't as fast as usual.

____

______________________________.'

5

Doreen Brooker lost her chance of winning £10,000 in prize money when her husband admitted forgetting to post her entry form. 'I'm not speaking to him,' said Doreen yesterday,

'______________________________

______________________________.'

6

Tommy Mangold lost his job at a car factory last week after making an unfortunate remark about his boss's wife. 'The trouble with Tommy is that he never thinks before he speaks,' said his mother.

'______________________________

______________________________.'

EXERCISE 10

It's two o'clock in the morning. Roger and Diana have just come back from a party. Complete the following dialogue by putting the verbs in brackets into the correct form. The first one has been done for you.

ROGER: Where's your key?

DIANA: What do you mean? You've got a key, haven't you?

ROGER: (1) If I **had got** (get) mine, I **wouldn't need** (not need) yours, would I?

DIANA: No, but I haven't got mine.

ROGER: But I told you to bring it.

DIANA: No, you didn't.

ROGER: Yes, I did. (2) If you ______________ (listen), you ______________ (hear) me.

DIANA: Well, I don't remember you telling me. Anyway, I couldn't find it.

ROGER: You mean you've lost it again?

DIANA: Not really. It's at home somewhere. (3) I ______________ (have) time to look for it if we ______________ (not leave) in such a hurry.

ROGER: That's not the point. (4) If you ______________ (be) more organised, you ______________ (keep on) losing it in the first place!

DIANA: That's not fair! I don't keep on losing it. Anyway, what are we going to do now? We haven't got a key.

ROGER: I don't know. I suppose I'll have to break a window.

DIANA: You can't do that! (5) If the neighbours ______________ (hear) you, they ______________ (think) we're burglars!

ROGER: All right, then. There's a small window open in the bathroom. (6) If you ______________ (stand) on my shoulders, you ______________ (be) able to reach it and then you can climb in.

DIANA: I'm not going to stand on your shoulders. I might fall off!

ROGER: Don't be silly! (7) If I ______________ (hold) your legs, you ______________ (be) quite safe.

DIANA: I still don't like it.

ROGER: Look. (8) I ______________ (climb) in myself if I ______________ (can) get through the window, but I can't. I'm too big. You'll have to do it.

DIANA: (9) But if someone ______________ (see) me, they ______________ (call) the police!

ROGER: For goodness sake! (10) It ________________ (make) things a lot easier if you ________________ (not worry) about other people! Now, are you ready?

DIANA: OK.

ROGER: All right?

DIANA: (11) If you ________________ (move) a bit closer, I ________________ (be) able to reach. Oh! Not so fast! Roger! Oh!!

ROGER: Now look what you've done! You've put your foot through the window!

DIANA: Roger, there's something I've got to tell you!

ROGER: Honestly, can't you do anything right! (12) If you ________________ (not be) so careless, you ________________ (break) it!

DIANA: Roger, listen! I hate to tell you, but this isn't our house!

EXERCISE 11

Use your own ideas to complete the following.

Example: You'd get a better photo **if you used a flash**.

1 If the weather improves, ________________.

2 If I knew the answer, ________________.

3 Take a message ________________.

4 If you'd asked me first, ________________.

5 Unless she works harder, ________________.

6 He wouldn't sell his car ________________.

7 Provided that you feel well enough, ________________.

8 If I'd known you were coming, ________________.

9 If you went to bed earlier, ________________.

10 It wouldn't have happened ________________.

17 INDIRECT (REPORTED) SPEECH

BIRD'S EYE BOX: Indirect (reported) speech

'I'm leaving on Friday.' **He says (that) he's leaving on Friday.**	→	introduced by present tense (Exercise 1)
'I'm leaving on Friday.' **He said (that) he was leaving on Friday.**	→	introduced by past tense (Exercises 2, 4 and 8)
'Can I give you a lift?' She **offered** to give them a lift.	→	verbs used to report speech (Exercise 3)
'I'll see you tomorrow.' He said (that) he would see her **the next/following day.**	→	time words in reported speech (Exercises 4 and 8)
'Are you going to the party?' **She asked me if/whether I was going to the party.**	→	reported questions (Exercises 5 and 8)
'When does it start?' **She asked me when it started.**		
'What shall I do?' **She asked me what to do.** **She asked me what she should do.**	→	reported questions with **to** + infinitive or modals (Exercise 6)
'Relax!' **He told her to relax.** **He told her (that) she should relax.**	→	reported imperative (Exercises 7 and 8)
'Don't worry!' **He told her not to worry.** **He told her (that) she shouldn't worry.**		

EXERCISE 1

Read the postcard and then complete the dialogue below. It is not necessary to repeat 'He says' every time. The first one has been done for you.

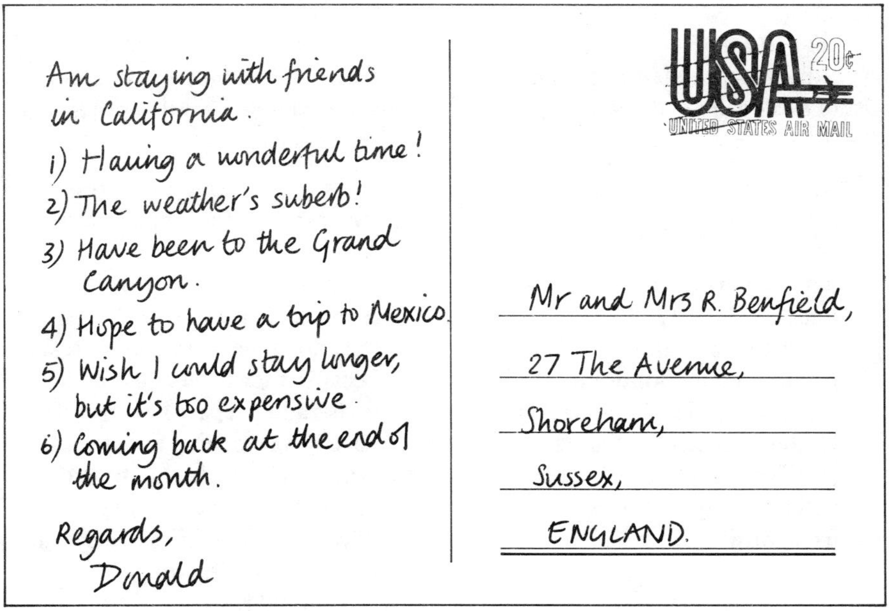

PENNY: Who's the postcard from, Richard?

RICHARD: Donald. **He says (that) he's staying with friends in California.**

PENNY: How lovely!

RICHARD: Yes. (1) He says ______________________.

PENNY: I'm sure he is.

RICHARD: (2) ______________________.

PENNY: And?

RICHARD: (3) ______________________.

PENNY: Lucky Donald!

RICHARD: And, listen to this! (4) ______________________.

PENNY: How exciting!

RICHARD: (5) ______________________.

PENNY: How long is he staying there?

RICHARD: (6) ______________________.

EXERCISE 2

Read both interviews and then complete the newspaper report below. The first one has been done for you.

INTERVIEWER: As Minister of Education, what do you think of the teachers' demand for a ten per cent pay rise? MINISTER: (1) Frankly, I have little sympathy for the teachers. (2) They are extremely lucky to have a short working day and long holidays. (3) The Government is not prepared to pay them more for doing nothing. (4) The Teachers' Union must accept that fact. (5) If they go on strike, they will be acting totally irresponsibly.	REPORTER: As leader of the Teachers' Union, what is your reaction to the Minister's remarks? LEADER OF THE TEACHERS' UNION: (6) I am extremely angry at the Minister's remarks. (7) Teachers are hard-working, responsible people. (8) When they go home, they cannot relax because they have to mark books and prepare lessons. (9) I have been teaching for twenty years, and during that time the pay and conditions have gone down. (10) The Minister has no idea what he's talking about and should resign!

Minister Unsympathetic Towards Teachers

In a television interview last night, the Minister of Education (1) **said (that) he had little sympathy for the teachers**.

(2) He said ____________________.

(3) ____________________.

(4) ____________________.

(5) ____________________.

When asked to comment on the Minister's remarks, Tom Bollard, leader of the Teachers' Union, said (6) ____________________.

(7) ____________________.

(8) ____________________.

(9) ____________________.

(10) ____________________.

EXERCISE 3

Decide which would be the most suitable reporting verb from the box below to report each of the following sentences. The first one has been done for you.

admit advise agree announce apologise demand offer promise suggest thank threaten warn

1 'I want to know where you've been!' **demand**

2 'I'm terribly sorry I'm late.' ______________

3 'I'll carry that case for you if you like.' ______________

4 'Don't touch that switch. It's dangerous.' ______________

5 'Well, if I were you, I'd see a doctor about it.' ______________

6 'It was very kind of you to look after the baby for me. I'm very grateful.' ______________

7 'We've decided to get married.' ______________

8 'Well, why don't we go by train?' ______________

9 'I really will pay you back tomorrow. Honestly!' ______________

10 'All right, I was breaking the speed limit.' ______________

11 'If you don't stop doing that immediately, I'll tell your father!' ______________

12 'Yes, you're right. It is difficult.' ______________

Now change each of the sentences into reported speech, using the correct reporting verb. You can choose which pronouns you want to use. The first one has been done for you.

1 **He demanded to know where she had been.**

2 ____.

3 ____.

4 ____.

5 ____.

6 ____.

7 ____.

8 ____.

9 ____.

10 ____.

11 ____.

12 ____.

EXERCISE 4

Read the following telephone conversation and then complete the letter below. The first one has been done for you.

'Sundridge Electrics. Can I help you?'
'I'd like to order a Bosch fridge-freezer.'
'I'm afraid (1) we sold the last one yesterday and (2) we haven't any more in stock now. But (3) we're expecting a delivery later on today. (4) They'll be here about three o'clock this afternoon. If you like, (5) I'll phone you and (6) we'll deliver one tomorrow.'

> Dear Sir,
>
> Two weeks ago I telephoned your shop to order a Bosch fridge-freezer. The assistant I spoke to told me (1) **that you had sold the last one the day before** and (2) that ______________________________. However, he informed me (3) that ______________________________ and (4) that ______________________________. He then said (5) that ______________________________ and (6) that ______________________________. Since then I have heard nothing more. Would you kindly let me know if these fridge-freezers are now in stock.
>
> Yours faithfully,
>
> *William Johnson*

EXERCISE 5

Recently you had an interview at an employment agency. Below are the questions you were asked. Read the questions and then complete the exercise that follows.

1 What experience have you had?
2 Can you type, write shorthand and use a telex machine?
3 Have you got any qualifications?
4 Why did you leave your last job?

5 How long have you been looking for another job?
6 Do you want to work in an office again?
7 Are you looking for a full-time or a part-time job?
8 When can you start work?

Example: Have you worked before?
She asked me if/whether I had/(I'd) worked before.

What are you interested in doing?
She asked me what I was interested in doing.

1 First of all, she asked me ______________________.
2 Then ______________________.
3 And then ______________________.
4 Next ______________________.
5 And after that ______________________.
6 Then ______________________.
7 And then ______________________.
8 Finally ______________________.

EXERCISE 6

Sheila runs an advice column in a weekly magazine. Read the following letters and then complete the exercise below.

1

I have to make a speech at my daughter's wedding. What shall I say?

Derek

2

I want to complain about the postal service. Who should I write to?

Valerie

3

I'm going to my husband's office party. What should I wear?

Sylvia

4

My son is having problems learning to read. How can I help him?

Jennifer

5

I need some legal advice, but I can't afford a solicitor. Where shall I go?

David

6

My daughter can't stop biting her nails. How can I stop her?

Margaret

Example:

> My life is being made miserable by my noisy neighbours. What can I do?
>
> Paul

Paul asked her what to do about his noisy neighbours.

or **Paul asked her what he could do about his noisy neighbours.**

1 Derek ______________________________.

2 Valerie ______________________________.

3 Sylvia ______________________________.

4 Jennifer ______________________________.

5 David ______________________________.

6 Margaret ______________________________.

EXERCISE 7

Tim is very unhappy with his landlady. Read what the landlady says and then complete the dialogue below.

1 Stay in your room after dinner!
2 Eat your meals in the kitchen, not the dining-room!
3 Don't bring your friends to the house!
4 Don't use the telephone!
5 Take your shoes off when you come indoors!
6 Don't make a noise after nine o'clock!
7 Don't use the bathroom after 8.00 p.m!
8 Smoke in the garden, not the house!

Example: 'Take your washing to the launderette!'
She told me to take my washing to the launderette.
or **She told me (that) I should/must take my washing to the launderette.**

'Don't use my washing machine!'
She told me not to use her washing machine.
or **She told me (that) I shouldn't/couldn't use her washing machine.**

TIM: I must find somewhere else to live. My landlady's impossible!

BOB: Why?

TIM: She's so unfriendly. You know, she told me (1) ______________________________.

BOB: Really?

TIM: Yes, and she (2) ______________________________.

BOB: You mean, by yourself?

TIM: Yes. But that's not all. (3) ______________________________.

BOB: She sounds awful!

TIM: She is. The day I arrived, (4) ______________________________.

BOB: Oh, dear!

TIM: And (5) ______________________________.

BOB: Your shoes!

TIM: Yes! Then (6) ______________________________.

BOB: Incredible!

TIM: But listen to this! (7) ______________________________.

BOB: I don't believe it!

TIM: It's true! And, finally, (8) ______________________________.

BOB: Well, I'm not surprised you want to move!

EXERCISE 8

Read the following extract from a board meeting of **Discoverer Lines,** *a shipping company. Then complete the minutes of the meeting below. The first one has been done for you.*

DIRECTOR: Right. (1) There are two ships we have to discuss this morning: the *Magellan* and the *Columbus*. (2) Mr McManus, is there any more news about the *Columbus*?

MR MCMANUS: (3) I had another telex from the captain yesterday. (4) The ship's still in Sydney Harbour and can't be unloaded because of the dockers' strike.

MR WATES: (5) Could the crew on the *Columbus* unload the ship themselves?

MR MCMANUS: No, (6) it's out of the question. (7) The Union would stop every ship in the company!

DIRECTOR: Well, (8) let me know as soon as you have any news, Mr McManus. Now, (9) I understand there's a problem with the *Magellan*. (10) What do you know about it, Mr Greaves?

MR GREAVES: (11) The *Magellan* broke down in the Mediterranean two days ago. (12) We're going to take the ship into Malta for repairs.

DIRECTOR: (13) How long will the repairs take?

MR GREAVES: (14) They shouldn't take longer than two or three days, but we may have to wait for spare parts.

DIRECTOR: (15) How much will the repairs cost, Mr Wates?

MR WATES: (16) I've got an estimate for $20,000, but that doesn't include the port charges.

DIRECTOR: (17) Are you planning to supervise the repairs yourself, Mr Greaves?

MR GREAVES: (18) Yes. My flight to Malta leaves tomorrow morning.

Discoverer Lines

Minutes of meeting held on Tuesday, 29 March

1 The Director **said (that) there were two ships they had to discuss that morning: the *Magellan* and the *Columbus*.**

2 He asked Mr McManus ____________________.

3 Mr McManus ____________________.

4 He ____________________.

5 Mr Wates ____________________.

6 Mr McManus ____________________.

7 He ____________________.

8 The Director ____________________.

9 He ____________________.

10 He ____________________.

11 Mr Greaves ____________________.

12 He ____________________.

13 The Director ____________________.

14 Mr Greaves ____________________.

15 The Director ____________________.

16 Mr Wates ____________________.

17 The Director ____________________.

18 Mr Greaves ____________________.

18 PREPOSITIONS

BIRD'S EYE BOX: Prepositions

Wait for me **outside** the cinema.	→	place (Exercises 1, 2, 7 and 8)
He worked **from** 9.00 **to** 5.00.	→	time (Exercises 3, 4, 7 and 8)
Everyone is here **except** Terry.	→	other prepositions, prepositional phrases (Exercises 5, 7 and 8)
There's nothing to **worry about**.	→	verb + preposition (Exercises 6, 7 and 8)

EXERCISE 1

Use the picture to help you complete the second part of the short dialogues. Choose a suitable preposition from the box below, but do not use any preposition more than once. The first one has been done for you.

across	behind	between	in	near	next to	on	opposite	outside

1 'Excuse me. Is there a car-park near here?'
'Yes, there's one **behind the supermarket**.'

2 'I wonder where I can change some money.'
'I think there's a bank ____________________.'

3 'Excuse me. I'm looking for a chemist's.'
'Well, the nearest one is ____________________.'

4 'Is there anywhere I can post a letter?'
'Yes, there's a letter-box ____________________.'

5 'I'd like to join the library, if there is one.'
'Oh, yes, there's a library ____________________.'

6 'Do you know where I can catch a bus to Harwich?'
'Yes, the bus stop's ____________________.'

EXERCISE 2

Use the map to complete the notice using suitable prepositions. The clues you need are in the map. Occasionally there may be more than one correct answer. The first one has been done for you.

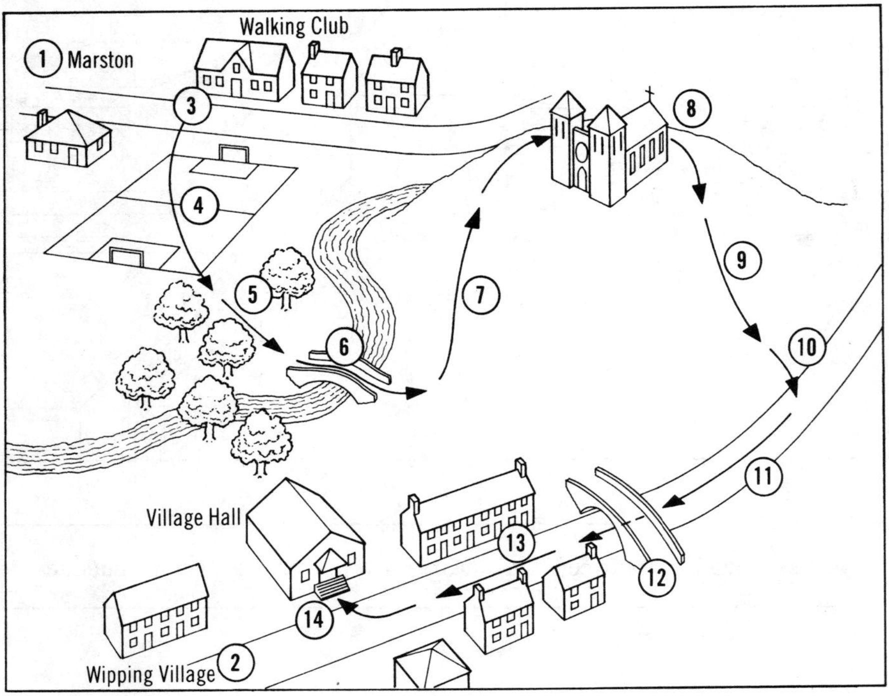

Marston Walking Club

There will be an eight-mile walk on Saturday afternoon (1) **from** Marston (2) ______________ Wipping Village. Walkers should meet (3) ______________ the club at two o'clock. The route is as follows. Go (4) ______________ the playing field, (5) ______________ Woyden's Wood and (6) ______________ the bridge. Then walk (7) ______________ Hollis Hill, (8) ______________ the church and (9) ______________ the hill again (10) ______________ the main road. Go (11) ______________ the main road, (12) ______________ the bridge and (13) ______________ the centre of Wipping Village. The walk will finish (14) ______________ the village hall. Anyone interested should sign below.

EXERCISE 3

Complete the following shop notices with the correct preposition. The first one has been done for you.

1

Sale starts **on** Monday!

2

Closed for lunch ______________ 1.00 and 2.00 p.m.

3

Late night shopping. Open ______________ 8.00 p.m. ______________ Thursdays.

4

Closing-down sale. Everything must go ______________ the end of the week.

5

Gone for lunch. Back ______________ two o'clock.

6

New Sellalot Supermarket opening ______________ January!

7

Havstock will be open ______________ 9.00 p.m. ______________ Sales Week!

8

Open ______________ 9.00 a.m. ______________ 5.30 p.m.

EXERCISE 4

A member of parliament is talking to his secretary. Complete the following dialogue with the correct prepositions. The first one has been done for you.

M. P.: Right, Simon, what's the programme?

SIMON: Rather busy, I'm afraid, sir. There's a meeting tomorrow (1) at nine o'clock, which will probably go on (2) ______________ lunchtime. Then (3) ______________ lunch you've got an appointment with the Prime Minister. She's expecting you (4) ______________ 2.15 and 2.30. Incidentally, the Foreign Secretary would like a word with you sometime (5) ______________ the afternoon.

M. P.: The Foreign Secretary? But I thought he was flying to Paris (6) ______________ the morning.

SIMON: He was, sir, but that visit's been cancelled because of the French elections. He's now going (7) ______________ July instead, but no one knows exactly when.

M. P.: Oh, I see. What else?

SIMON: Well, (8) ______________ Thursday you've got another meeting, which is scheduled to last (9) ______________ 10.00 a.m. (10) ______________ 12.00 p.m. Oh, and I almost forgot, the Home Secretary wants to see you (11) ______________ the meeting starts. He said it wouldn't take long.

M. P.: I wonder what he wants.

SIMON: I think it's something to do with your visit to Manchester (12) ______________ the 23rd.

M. P.: Oh, right. Any news from Sir Harold yet?

SIMON: Nothing definite, sir. I phoned his secretary earlier and, apparently, Sir Harold's been out of the country (13) ______________ the last few days. I said you had to have an answer (14) ______________ Friday at the latest, and he's promised to let you know (15) ______________ twenty-four hours.

M. P.: I see.

SIMON: Oh, and one last thing, sir. The television people have been waiting to see you (16) ______________ three o'clock.

M. P.: What do they want?

SIMON: Well, if you remember, you're doing a party political broadcast (17) ______________ two days' time.

M. P.: Am I? Good heavens, I'd completely forgotten about it! Show them in immediately. This is important!

EXERCISE 5

Use the word or words in brackets to complete the second sentence so that it means the same as the first.

Example: The only person who didn't come to the party was Jane. (apart from)
Everyone came to the party apart from Jane.

1 She used a knife to open the parcel.
She opened ________________. (with)

2 The Labour Party believes that nuclear weapons are wrong.
The Labour Party is ________________. (against)

3 He was in pain, but he managed to finish the race.
He managed to ________________. (in spite of)

4 No one helped him solve the problem.
He solved ________________. (by)

5 Unemployment is going down, or so the Government says.
Unemployment ________________. (according to)

6 Barbara's the only person I've told.
I haven't ________________. (except)

7 He didn't think before he spoke.
He spoke ________________. (without)

8 Is French the only foreign language she speaks?
Does she speak ________________. (besides)

9 Tom and a friend share a flat.
Tom shares ________________. (with)

10 Penny married Alec, although her parents disapproved.
Penny married ________________. (despite)

11 We can only accept a cheque if you have a cheque card.
We can't ________________. (without)

12 The only thing I haven't done is clean the bathroom.
I've done ________________. (apart from)

EXERCISE 6

Annie Moss writes an advice column in a magazine. Complete the following letters by choosing the appropriate verb, putting it in the correct form and combining it with the correct preposition from the boxes below. The first one has been done for you.

1

talk think be interested get bored

with in at of about

Dear Annie,

My boyfriend (a) **is** only **interested in** football and he never (b) ______ ______ anything else. Quite honestly, I'm (c) ______ ______ his conversation. We were (d) ______ ______ getting married, but now I'm not so sure. What do you think?

Paula

2

believe worry agree shout

about on at for in

Dear Annie,

I'm very (a) ______ ______ my son and his wife. They are always (b) ______ ______ each other and don't seem able to (c) ______ ______ anything. Personally, I don't (d) ______ divorce, but they are obviously not happy together. Do you think I should say anything?

Betty

3

suffer think ask laugh

for from at in about

Dear Annie,

There's a girl in my office I find very attractive. In fact, I can't stop (a) ____________ ____________ her. The problem is, I (b) ____________ extreme shyness. I would like to (c) ____________ her ____________ a date, but I'm afraid she might (d) ____________ me. What do you think I should do?

Alan

4

get tired agree look complain

about of with for at

Dear Annie,

My boyfriend is very possessive. If I even (a) ____________ another boy, he gets very angry. I'm (b) ____________ ____________ the situation, but if I (c) ____________ his jealousy, he says I don't love him. I do love him, but I'm only seventeen and I want to enjoy myself. My mother thinks I should leave him. Do you (d) ____________ her?

Liza

EXERCISE 7

Alice Withers is teaching a class of difficult ten-year-olds. Complete the following with suitable prepositions. Sometimes there is more than one correct answer. The first one has been done for you.

Late again, Jimmy, I see. The lesson started (1) at three o'clock, if you remember. Never mind. Sit over there (2) ______________ Sandra, where I can see you. Now, what were we talking (3) ______________? Ah yes, who was the king of England (4) ______________ 1400? Doesn't anyone else know (5) ______________ Patrick? Tracey, what are you reading (6) ______________ your desk? No, it's no good trying to hide it (7) ______________ your back. I'm not blind. Comics should be read (8) ______________ the lesson, not (9) ______________ it. Come and put it (10) ______________ my desk, there's a good girl. Now, open your books (11) ______________ page 24. Jimmy, what are you doing (12) ______________ Sandra's book? Give it back to her at once. And don't look (13) ______________ me like that. It's your own fault if you've come to school (14) ______________ your books. Now, everyone, copy the picture (15) ______________ page 24, and I want you all to have finished it (16) ______________ the time the bell rings. Gary Browne, try and concentrate (17) ______________ the lesson. You've been looking (18) ______________ the window ever (19) ______________ the class started. And don't think I can't see you just because you're sitting (20) ______________ Thomas West. I think you'd better come and sit over here (21) ______________ me. Are you chewing gum, Gary? You know that's (22) ______________ the school rules. Go and throw it (23) ______________ the waste-paper basket immediately! Now, I don't want to hear another word from anyone (24) ______________ the bell rings. All right? Oh, dear, was that the bell? Right, you can all go home, (25) ______________ David Peters. I want to speak to you, David, (26) ______________ you leave.

EXERCISE 8

Complete the following news broadcast with the correct prepositions. The first one has been done for you.

Good evening, and here is the news.

The President of Romania arrived (1) in London this afternoon. He was met (2) ______________ Victoria Station (3) ______________ the Foreign Secretary. This is the first visit by a Romanian president (4) ______________ more than twelve years. He will be staying (5) ______________ the Romanian Consulate (6) ______________ Friday.

The Prime Minister, who has been suffering (7) ______________ a heavy cold, returned to work today. She said she felt much better, apart (8) ______________ a bad cough. She is to meet the American Secretary of State (9) ______________ Wednesday to talk (10) ______________ future trade agreements (11) ______________ the two countries.

Two jumbo jets narrowly missed each other when flying (12) ______________ the Channel (13) ______________ the weekend. The pilot of one aircraft said that he had to take emergency action when he saw the other aircraft coming (14) ______________ him. Several passengers were later treated (15) ______________ hospital (16) ______________ shock.

The £2 a week pay increase for nurses has been severely criticised (17) ______________ the Nurses' Union. Their spokesman, Tony Black, said, 'We had hoped (18) ______________ a much bigger increase, but, as usual, we have been disappointed. Nurses' incomes are far (19) ______________ the national average, and even (20) ______________ this increase we still won't have enough to live (21) ______________.'

Workmen pulling down a house (22) ______________ Wellington Road, Cheshire, have found a number of valuable Roman objects (23) ______________ the foundations. (24) ______________ these objects were several coins, which, according (25) ______________ the British Museum, are extremely rare.

A lioness escaped (26) ______________ Manchester Zoo early this morning. She jumped (27) ______________ her cage when her keeper opened the door to feed her. Residents living (28) ______________ the zoo were asked to stay (29) ______________ and to shut all doors and windows (30) ______________ the lioness was recaptured.

And here is Bill Jones with the weather forecast.

Good evening. Well, I hope you've had a good day (31) ______________ the weather! It's been very wet everywhere, and (32) ______________ some areas it has rained continuously (33) ______________ the day. However, the good news is that the rain should stop (34) ______________ the night and (35) ______________ the morning most of the clouds will have cleared away. Tomorrow will be a fine day, warm and sunny, with temperatures slightly (36) ______________ average for the time of year, (37) ______________ in coastal areas, where a cold wind (38) ______________ the sea will keep temperatures down.

19 PHRASAL VERBS

BIRD'S EYE BOX: Phrasal verbs

House prices must **come down** again.	→	one particle (Exercises 1, 4 and 5)
I don't **get on with** him very well.	→	two particles (Exercises 1, 4 and 5)
She's got over **the shock**. Take off **your coat**/Take **your coat** off.	→	position of object (Exercise 2)
She's got over **it**. Take **it** off.	→	position of pronoun (Exercises 3, 4 and 5)

EXERCISE 1

Complete the following by putting a circle round the correct word or words in the brackets. When you need to use two words, you should number them (1 and 2) to show the correct word order.

Examples: If you hold (back /(on)/ off) a minute, sir, I'll try and connect you.

He's too far ahead. We'll never catch ((with)[2]/ on /(up)[1]) him now!

1 When his car broke (in/out/down), he had to get the garage to repair it.

2 If you don't pay your phone bill, I'm afraid you'll be cut (off/up/out).

3 We're good friends now, but we didn't get (over/on/with) each other as children.

4 I see that Indian restaurant has closed (up/with/down). It didn't last long.

5 I'm terribly sorry I'm late. I ran (of/out/off) petrol on the way here.

6 Don't walk so fast! I can't keep (with/up/over) you!

7 I think I'd better set (of/up/off) a bit earlier tomorrow to miss the traffic.

8 Look at this letter from the bank manager! We've really got to cut (on/off/down) the amount we spend!

9 I had a terrible journey this morning. I was held (in/up/back) in the traffic for half an hour.

10 What time did you get (with/over/in) last night?

EXERCISE 2

Complete the following by choosing the appropriate phrasal verb and a suitable noun from the boxes below. If there are two possible positions for the noun, you should write both. Do not use any phrasal verb more than once.

Examples:

put off come up with	an idea our holiday

1 We were going away on Saturday, but we've had to

(a) **put our holiday off**
(b) **put off our holiday** for a couple of weeks.

2 We didn't know what to do about the problem until Nick

(a) **came up with an idea.**

(b) ____________.

carry on with fill in get on with look after make up run into run out of turn off	an excuse his father-in-law the lesson petrol the lights the baby this form an old friend

1 John likes his wife's mother, but he doesn't

(a) ____________________.

(b) ____________________.

2 It's very kind of you to (a) ____________________ while I'm (b) ____________________ out. I'm sure she won't be any trouble.

3 I really don't want to go to Ann's party. I'll have to

(a) ____________________.

(b) ____________________.

4 We'd better stop at a garage soon. We don't want to

(a) ____________________.

(b) ____________________.

5 Right, sir. If you'd like to join the club, could you

(a) ______________________________?

(b) ______________________________?

6 Sorry to interrupt. This won't take long, and then you can

(a) ______________________________.

(b) ______________________________.

EXERCISE 3

Complete the following by writing the correct alternative (a or b) in the box. The first one has been done for you.

1 I used to smoke, but I ______________ a few years ago
(a) gave it up (b) gave up it [a]

2 I've had a terrible cold, but fortunately I've nearly ______________.
(a) got it over (b) got over it [ ]

3 John's like his father, but Sheila ______________.
(a) takes me after (b) takes after me [ ]

4 What time shall I ______________?
(a) pick you up (b) pick up you [ ]

5 If you don't know what it means, ______________ in the dictionary.
(a) look it up (b) look up it [ ]

6 I rather like these trousers. Can I ______________?
(a) try them on (b) try on them [ ]

7 Look at this old diary. I ______________ in a second-hand bookshop.
(a) came it across (b) came across it [ ]

8 They offered me the job, but the money was so bad I ______________.
(a) turned it down (b) turned down it [ ]

9 Oh, you haven't lost your car keys again, have you? Well, this time I'm not helping you ______________.
(a) look them for (b) look for them [ ]

10 My father's in favour of capital punishment, but I ______________.
(a) am it against (b) am against it [ ]

EXERCISE 4

Complete the following with a pronoun and the correct particle or particles from the box below. Pay careful attention to the position of the pronoun.

back down forward of off on out to up with

Example: I wish I hadn't worn this thick sweater!
Well, take **it off**, then.

1 'Your television programme begins in a minute, dear.'
'Oh, could you turn ______________ for me, please?'

2 'You're going on holiday next week, aren't you?'
'Yes, we're going to Turkey. I'm really looking ______________.'

3 'All they ever talk about on television nowadays is the general election!'
'I know. I'm getting fed ______________!'

4 'Is Tom flying to Canada on Saturday?'
'Yes. We're going to the airport to see ______________.'

5 'Have you finished what you were doing?'
'No, but I can carry ______________ later.'

6 'How much do I owe you?'
'I'm not sure. I haven't worked ______________ yet.'

7 'Mummy! Look what I've got!'
'That's Barry's comic, not yours. Give ______________ to him at once!'

8 'Don't you want to go on holiday with Brenda now?'
'Not really, but I don't know how to get ______________.'

9 'Can't we do something about the noise from the road-works?'
'No, we can't. We'll just have to put ______________.'

10 'Awful weather, isn't it?
'Yes, it's so depressing. It really gets ______________.'

EXERCISE 5

Think of your own ideas to answer the following questions, using one of the phrasal verbs from the box below. Pay careful attention to any pronouns you may use. The first one has been done for you.

get in	get on with	get over	give back	give up	hold up	look for
look up	make up	take off	try on	turn off		

1 'Do you smoke?'
'Not any more. I've given it up.'

2 'Were you late again this morning?'
'____.'

3 'What do you think of the new secretary?'
'____.'

4 'How's your cold?'
'____.'

5 'Have you still got that book I lent you?'
'____.'

6 'Do you know Patricia's phone number?'
'____.'

7 'Can I help you?'
'____.'

8 'It's awfully hot in here, isn't it?'
'____.'

20 LINKING WORDS

BIRD'S EYE BOX: Linking words

It's bright **and** sunny **but** the wind's cold.	→	relationships (Exercises 1 and 9)
He left **before** the match finished.	→	time (Exercises 2 and 9)
I'll tell him **when I see him**.	→	future time, present tense (Exercises 3 and 9)
She's upset **because** he shouted at her.	→	reason (Exercises 4 and 9)
The children behaved **so** badly **(that)** their mother sent them to bed.	→	result (Exercises 5 and 9)
He got the job, **although** he wasn't qualified.	→	contrast (Exercises 6 and 9)
He went to the manager **to** ask for a pay rise.	→	purpose (Exercises 7 and 9)
It's not **as** easy **as** you think!	→	comparison (Exercises 8 and 9)

EXERCISE 1

Using ***and, but, either/or, neither/nor,*** join each of the following groups of two or three sentences to form one sentence. Then complete the advertisement below. The first one has been done for you.

1 It's warm. It's sunny.
2 The beaches are empty. The sea is clear blue.
3 It's not crowded. It's not commercialized.
4 Life is quiet. There's plenty to do.
5 You can rent an apartment. You can stay in a two-star hotel.
6 The accommodation isn't luxurious. It's clean. It's comfortable.
7 Phone 01 762 9292. Call into our offices.

Are you looking for a quiet, relaxing holiday away from the crowds? Are you interested in an island where (1) **it's warm and sunny** all the year round? Then come to Mandrake Island where (2) ______________________________!
(3) ______________________________ on Mandrake Island. (4) ______________________________ for those who want to get away from it all!

A two-week holiday costs from £250 per person. (5) ______________________________. (6) ______________________________ Interested?

For more details you can (7) ______________________________.

EXERCISE 2

Complete the extract from a letter of application by using the linking words in the box to join the following notes. There is often more than one possible answer, but you should use each word or phrase once only. The first one has been done for you.

after	as soon as	before	since	until	when	while

1 Left school in 1976. Went to Italy for six months.
2 Returned to England. Then applied for three-year architectural course.
3 Studying at Manchester University. Developed an interest in photography.
4 Left the university in April 1980. Didn't take final exams in June.
5 Worked for advertising agency. Saved enough money.
6 Qualified. Have been employed by the *Daily News*.
7 Contract finishes in April. Shall be immediately available to start a new job.

(1) **After leaving school in 1976, I went to Italy for six months** to study architecture. (2) ______________________________ at Manchester University. (3) ______________________________, and so (4) ______________________________.

I came to London and (5) ______________________________

________________________ to start a two-year diploma course in photography at Hampden College of Fine Arts, which I completed in 1983. (6) ________________________ as a sports photographer. However, (7) ________________________

________________________.

EXERCISE 3

Expand the notes in the brackets to complete the second part of the following short dialogues.

Example: 'I'd like a word with you, Mary.'
'OK. **I'll see you when the lesson finishes**.'
(I/see/you when/the lesson/finish)

1 'I hope I won't be too long.'
'Don't hurry. ________________________.'
(I/look/after the children/until/you/get/back)

2 'Don't be too late, dear.'
'No, I won't. ________________________.'
(As soon as/the programme/end/I/come/to bed)

3 'I'm afraid Tom's out. Can I take a message?'
'Well, ________________________?'
(you/ask/him to phone me/when/he/come/in?)

4 'I hate flying! I'm always airsick!'
'Never mind. ________________________.'
(Once/the plane/land/you/feel/much better.)

5 'You might need to put some more oil in the car, Derek.'
'Don't worry. ________________________.'
(I/check/it/before/I/go/out)

6 'I've just got to cash a cheque.'
'OK. ________________________.'
(I/wait/in the car/while/you/be/in the bank?)

EXERCISE 4

Join the following ideas by choosing one of the linking words or phrases in the box below. Do not change the order of the sentences. There is often more than one possible answer, but you should use each word or phrase once only.

as	because	because of	since	that's why	that's the reason why

Example: He was offered a better job. He left.
He was offered a better job. That's why he left.

1 I couldn't phone you last night. I left your number at work.
2 The flight was delayed. There was snow on the runway.
3 The train was cancelled. I was late.
4 He failed his driving test. He didn't stop at the red lights.
5 I'd better meet him at the station. He doesn't know the way.
6 It was far too expensive. I didn't buy it.

EXERCISE 5

Use the words in brackets to link together the following notes. (Sometimes you may still need to have two separate sentences.) Then complete the letter of complaint below. The first one has been done for you.

1 Men did a lot of damage. Will now have to replace table and two chairs. (such . . . that)

2 China and glass packed badly. A number of valuable pieces were broken. (so . . . that)

3 Men refused to carry any heavy furniture upstairs. Had to carry it myself. (so . . . that)

4 Injured my back. Have had to take a week off work. (as a result, consequently)

5 Should receive some compensation for damage and inconvenience. Have written to my solicitor. (therefore)

Dear Sir,

Ref: Removal of furniture to 8 Windermere Road

I am writing to complain about the service provided by your removal company when I moved house last Wednesday.

In the first place, (1) **the men did such a lot of damage that I will now have to replace a table and two chairs.**
Secondly, (2) ____

____

In addition, (3) ____

______________________________. (4) ______________________

and ____.

I am extremely dissatisfied with your company and feel strongly that (5) ____________________. ____________________

______________ who will contact you within the next few days.

Yours faithfully,

T. Booth

EXERCISE 6

Complete the following dialogue by choosing the appropriate word or phrase from the box below. Use each once only. The first one has been done for you.

whereas	while	however	even though	on the other hand
but	although			

INTERVIEWER: What do you think Spicer's chances are of winning the championship? After all, he's only fourteen.

COACH: Well, I think his chances are very good, (1) **even though** he's so young. He's an extremely promising player.

INTERVIEWER: (2) ____________________ he doesn't have much experience, does he?

COACH: That's true. (3) ____________________ he's extremely enthusiastic and has lots of energy, which is very important.

INTERVIEWER: What about strength? Aren't the older players much stronger than he is?

COACH: Well, I was a little worried about that at first. (4) ______________________, it doesn't seem to make a great deal of difference. You see, (5) ______________________ other players have strength, Spicer has speed. He's extremely fast on his feet and extremely accurate too.

INTERVIEWER: So you think he's definitely a name to watch?

COACH: Oh, certainly. I'm confident that he'll do very well, (6) ______________________ he may not win the title this year.

EXERCISE 7

Use the words in brackets to link together the ideas in the following pairs of sentences. You will have to think of a suitable verb to complete the second part of the sentence. (There is sometimes more than one acceptable answer.)

Example: He hated arguments. So he kept his opinions to himself. (in order not to) **He kept his opinions to himself in order not to start an argument.**

1 She'd booked a holiday in America. So she had to get a visa. (to)

2 I don't want her card to arrive late. So I'll post it early. (so that)

3 He was away from his family a lot. So he gave up his career in the navy. (in order to)

4 His flatmate was asleep. So he turned his radio down. (so as not to)

5 They thought their children might not have a very good future in Britain. So they decided to emigrate to Australia. (in order that)

6 She didn't have many friends. So she joined a club. (so as to)

EXERCISE 8

Adam Waring writes a good food guide in a monthly magazine. Use the notes he made on his first and second visit to Vicino's restaurant to complete the article below. Use **as . . . as** *or* **not as . . . as** *in your answers. The first one has been done for you.*

First visit

1 Menu: choice of 8 dishes
2 Food: very well cooked
3 Service: efficient
4 waiters friendly
5 Atmosphere: relaxed
6 Prices: £20–£30 per person
7 General impression: very good

Second visit

1 Menu: choice of 8 dishes
2 Food: quite well cooked
3 Service: efficient
4 waiters friendly
5 Atmosphere: less relaxed
6 Prices: £15–£25 per person
7 General impression: quite good

Eat with Adam

This week I paid a second visit to Vicino's in Soho. Since I last ate there, the management has changed, so I was interested to see what it was like. There was still (1) **as much** choice on the menu **as** before, but the food was (2) ____________ the last time I ate there. The service was just (3) ____________ ____________ previously, and the waiters were still (4) ____________ ____________ I remembered them. However, the atmosphere, though pleasant, was (5) ____________ on my first visit. On the other hand, the prices were (6) ____________ before. Generally, I was a little disappointed as it was (7) ____________ I expected.

EXERCISE 9

Below is an extract from a chairman's speech to the Board of Directors. Complete each of the spaces with a suitable linking word. Where there is more than one possibility, try to use as many different words as possible. The first one has been done for you.

As you all know, we have been through an economic crisis recently and, (1) **as a result**, we have not made (2) ____________ much profit ____________ we did last year. The figures for this year are £2.5 million, (3) ____________ last year our profits came to more than £6 million. (4) ____________, we have had to reduce the workforce in some areas, and (5) ____________ we decided,

reluctantly, to close down the Bromsgrove factory
(6) ______________ it had been making a loss for some time.

(7) ______________ there is some good news.
(8) ______________ increase sales in the Far East, we are, at present, negotiating a contract with Japan. These negotiations are in the early stages, (9) ______________ I am confident that a contract will be signed. Obviously, I will let you know (10) ______________ I have any definite news.

On a personal note, we are very sorry to say goodbye to one of our directors, Ernest Smith, who is taking early retirement (11) ______________ ill health. He has been with the company (12) ______________ it was formed in 1963. Brian Waite will be taking over as director, and I trust everyone will be (13) ______________ co-operative ______________ possible (14) ______________ he can familiarise himself with the company. The date for our next board meeting still has to be fixed. It will (15) ______________ be at the end of July (16) ______________ the beginning of September, (17) ______________ I have to visit Japan in August. You will be told (18) ______________ the date is definite.

21 PUNCTUATION

BIRD'S EYE BOX: Punctuation

My name's Pedro and I come from Mexico.	→	capital letters (Exercises 1, 2 and 5)
I've asked Jim, Pat and Dick, but not Sandra.	→	commas, full stops (Exercises 2 and 5)
Can I help you? Do be quiet!	→	question marks, exclamation marks (Exercises 3 and 5)
'I'll be in the Teachers' Room,' she said.	→	quotation marks, apostrophes (Exercises 3 and 5)
Trivial: of small value; commonplace.	→	colon, semicolon (Exercises 4 and 5)
I hear Peter (Mary's ex-husband) is getting married again – at least, Mary says so.	→	brackets, hyphens, dashes (Exercises 4 and 5)

EXERCISE 1

Correct the following by putting in capital letters where necessary.

1 i'm meeting brenda at victoria station on saturday afternoon. we'll probably do some shopping in bond street before going to the theatre in shaftesbury avenue.

2 sir richard algrave has been appointed british ambassador to brazil. he is well qualified for the position, having studied south american history at oxford university, as well as being a fluent portuguese speaker. he is due to take up the appointment after christmas.

3 what does scotland have to offer the tourist, besides the loch ness monster? well, how about a climb in the grampian mountains or a boat trip across to the isle of skye? interested? we're offering cut-price holidays in september. for more details contact highland tours, 136 regent street, london w 4.

EXERCISE 2

Punctuate the following by putting in commas and full stops where necessary. Remember you will need to put a capital letter at the beginning of a new sentence.

1 Unfortunately Prof Maurice Spitz is unable to give tonight's lecture however we are very pleased to welcome Dr Edmund Johnston instead Dr Johnston as many of you will know is an expert in Middle Eastern affairs

2 Certain foods e g eggs milk cheese butter etc are unhealthy if eaten in large quantities on the other hand bread and potatoes traditionally considered fattening are very important in a healthy diet

3

West Worth Co Ltd

The company's annual dinner and dance will be held at the Queen's Hotel Wallace Rd Epsom on Sat Dec 5th at 800 p m

EXERCISE 3

Punctuate the following by putting in the necessary quotation marks, apostrophes, question marks and exclamation marks.

1 The man walked into the bank and pulled out a gun.
Hands up he shouted. Dont move
What do you want the bank manager asked, knowing very well what the answer would be.
What do you think replied the man coldly. Now give me the keys to the safe

2 Help
What was that asked Toby.
I didnt hear anything, his friend Gerry replied.
I thought I heard someone call help. It sounded like a womans voice.
Listen There it is again Come on, lets see whats wrong

3 Ray and Eddy watched in astonishment as Paul stopped the Porsche outside Eddys house.
What a fantastic car said Ray.
Where did you get it asked Eddy.
Paul enjoyed seeing the look of astonishment on his friends faces.
Its my brothers car, he said. Hes lent it to me while hes away.
You lucky thing said Ray. Can we have a go

EXERCISE 4

Below is the introduction to a book on vegetable growing. Make the extract clearer by adding brackets, dashes, hyphens, colons and semicolons where you think appropriate.

Vegetables are for everyone not just vegetarians! And yet we, the British, eat fewer vegetables annually eighty five kilos per person than most other Europeans. However, this may all change now that more people are becoming interested in growing their own.

Home grown vegetables have three definite advantages over shop bought ones you can choose the kinds of vegetables you wish to grow you can pick and eat them the moment they are ready you can save money not to mention the satisfaction of having grown them yourself!

In this book we have included thirty five different types of vegetables. Some are old favourites carrots, lettuces, potatoes while others are less well known. And, in addition, we have included a special section on growing herbs pages 116–19.

Which vegetables you choose to grow the old favourites or something new is entirely up to you.

EXERCISE 5

Punctuate the following letter and newspaper article correctly.

1

dear bill

congratulations i hear youve been promoted to managing director how about meeting for lunch to celebrate well be away for a week in mid aug the annual visit to my mother in laws home in ireland but well be back on the twenty fourth why dont you give me a ring so we can arrange something

regards

terry

p s dont know if youve got my new number its 743 9631 ext 41

2

residents of banbury road ipswich are angry about yesterdays decision by the local council to allow the sunday market in banbury road to continue the residents havė three main complaints the excessive noise from 700 a m every sunday the increase in traffic which endangers childrens lives one child was knocked down last month the amount of litter in the street after the market closes

mrs hilda west who has lived in the road for more than twenty five years said im furious its all right for the councillors they dont have to live here this used to be a quiet road before the market arrived

the residents now plan to write to their local m p william davis the council refused to comment on their decision